Blue is the Color of Heaven:

The Story of a Boy's Love, Strength & Beyond

Shared by his Warrior Mom

Dana Ziemniak

Aurora Corialis Publishing

Pittsburgh, PA

Blue is the Color of Heaven: The Story of a Boy's Love, Strength & Beyond

Copyright © 2022 by Dana Ziemniak

All external reference links utilized in this book have been validated to the best of our ability and are current as of publication.

Printed in the United States of America

Edited by: Renee Picard, Aurora Corialis Publishing

Cover Design: Karen Captline, BetterBe Creative

Paperback ISBN: 978-1-958481-96-7

Ebook ISBN: 978-1-958481-97-4

Dedication

Pictured: Evan and Kit Kat

Evan William Ziemniak

January 15, 2004 – March 23, 2016

This book is dedicated to my son and all the other beautiful children gone too soon, always loved and never forgotten. Evan may have only been here for a short time, but he has made a huge impact and a lasting impression on others. He has taught me to be kinder and more compassionate and to never judge others. He has shown me that love never dies, and our spirits live on. Over the years, he has continued to do wonderful things and help others. I am so very proud of him, and I am forever blessed that he chose me to be his mother.

Praise for *Blue is the Color of Heaven*

"A must read for every parent or anyone who knows a parent!

"Dana Ziemniak has painted a picture of her beautiful son Evan and the tragedy that befell their whole family as a result of this activity. It is heartwarming and heartbreaking at the same time.

"Having lost my own son to the same 'game,' I thoroughly understand what she has done and why. I applaud her for her courage and fearlessness in sharing her story in such detail. Despite all the work I've done over the years to spread awareness and education to prevent further deaths from this activity, I don't know that I would have the same mettle to share as deeply as Dana did. Kudos!"

~ Judy Rogg, Director of Erik's Cause

~

"*Blue is the Color of Heaven* is a resource for educators, parents, and health care professionals. Her appeal to awareness, justice, and healing is evident as part of her healing progress. Not one more child, family, or community should have to have this reality, and she shows valiancy."

~ Francine D. Pritt, MS, LPC, NCC

~

"A beautifully written true story about a mother's love and survival after child loss. As a mother who has experienced a heartbreak and devastation after losing my own daughter, I can relate to Dana's story on so many levels. Dana's brutal honesty about her feelings and struggles makes her story very powerful. It's very sad, of course, but it will educate people and change their perspective on life.

"As a grief coach, I'm very proud of Dana for making such huge progress in moving forward in the grieving process. From my own experience of writing books, I know how therapeutic that is. *Blue is the Color of Heaven* is such a beautiful tribute to her son Evan, and as a huge believer in the spirit world, I know for sure that he is very proud of his strong and beautiful mother."

~ Elly Sheykhet | Vice President of Alina's Light, *Author of One Year After: From Grief to Hope* and *The Beauty of a Grieving Mother: Mothers Share their Stories of Finding Hope after the Loss of a Child*

~

"*Blue is the Color of Heaven* is an impactful and heart-wrenching story that encourages stalwart persistence despite incredible difficulty and unfathomable loss. With a call to action to make the world a place where everyone is valued through kindness, compassion, and doing what's right, Ziemniak tenderly conveys the hard reality that there is hope, joy, and pain in realizing the spirit of love never dies."

~ Amy Hooper Hanna & Holly Joy McIlwain, Co-authors of *For She Who Grieves: Practical Wisdom for Living Hope*

Table of Contents

Introduction...i

Chapter 1.. 1

Chapter 2 9

Chapter 3 21

Chapter 4 41

Chapter 5 59

Chapter 6 89

Chapter 7.. 101

Chapter 8 111

Chapter 9 123

Chapter 10.. 133

A Call to Action 147

Introduction

I am the mother of two beautiful children. One lives here on earth, and the other in heaven. I have never been a writer, but I felt drawn to write a book and share my son's story and my story of survival. My wish is to bring hope to anyone living with child loss or anyone struggling with the challenges of raising a child with disabilities. I know how hard both situations are and how lonely it can feel at times. I hope that this book will bring strength and encouragement to others to keep going and warrior on.

My husband Matt and I were married in 1999. We had our son, Evan, in 2004 and then our daughter, Ava, in 2009. We had everything we ever wanted until the tragic day in 2016 when we lost our son. To say our lives were demolished is an understatement, but somehow, we have managed to keep going. We now live for our daughter and to keep Evan's memory alive.

My story is a multifaceted one that includes raising a child with disabilities, fighting to get answers, and then fighting to get help and appropriate services for my child in school. It also includes the incompetence of a school and the bullying that led to the death of my son. To this day, I continue to fight for my son and for others like him and to spread awareness about the deadly pass-out challenge that took his life and continues to take the lives of other children.

My husband and I had never heard of the pass-out game prior to losing our son, so we were not able to warn him of the dangers. Now, we are all too familiar with it, so we want to pass along our knowledge in hopes of saving another family from the nightmare we are living. Evan has said that I need to stay here and save lives so I will do my best and honor him. Helping others gives me a purpose and it helps me in my grief as well.

Anyone who has ever lost a child knows that your emotions can be all over the place. One minute you can feel great sadness and despair, and the next you can feel extreme anger. Some days I feel okay and manage to get things done, and other days, it's all I can do to just exist. My husband and I do our very best to make sure Ava has the best life she can. We want her to know that she is just as important to us as Evan is, but it's hard. It's hard to grieve a child and take care of another child. Not only did she lose her brother, but she also lost the parents she had when her brother was alive.

Ava has coped well over the years, considering what we have all been through. Early on, she struggled as one would expect. She was only six years old at the time of Evan's death, so she didn't fully understand what had happened. She understood that he wasn't coming back and that her parents were different and sad.

As I wrote this book, Ava was the same age Evan was when we lost him. As the years have passed by, her memories of Evan have faded. She has some memories of him and the day we lost him, but she doesn't remember things the way we do. It's heartbreaking, but it's also a blessing because she doesn't have all the pain that her father and I carry.

We keep Evan very present in our lives. Not a day goes by that we don't talk about him and share memories. I can smile and laugh more now, but I still cry. I always will. It's important for me to be able to talk about Evan and share him with others. I love when people say his name and share their own memories of him. It's worth the tears to be able to know that Evan is still remembered and loved.

Many people have told me that I am strong, but I do not feel that way at all. I was never given a choice to do anything other than to carry on and find another way to continue to have a relationship with my son. It is not easy, and I would prefer to have him back with me, but I am so grateful for all the signs and messages. They bring me hope and the knowledge that Evan is still very much alive and with me and that one day we will be together again.

This is Evan's story ...

Chapter 1

It all began in April of 2003 when I found out I was pregnant with our first baby. We were so excited and full of hopes and dreams at the start of our new journey, but we ended up with more questions than answers. We thought we were so prepared for this next chapter of our lives, but little did we know there was nothing that could've prepared us.

We decided not to tell anyone our happy news until after we saw the doctor. Finally, the day of my first doctor's appointment arrived. They did an ultrasound but were unable to find the heartbeat. The doctor said it was possible that my dates were off, but most likely the baby never formed. He wanted to see me again in two weeks to double-check but warned me that most likely I would need a D&C procedure. My husband, Matt, and I were devastated. I had already become attached to this baby and looked forward to being a mother. At the time, this was the worst I had ever felt.

We went out of town that weekend for my soon-to-be sister-in-law's wedding shower. It was so hard trying to hide my sadness from everyone. I just wanted to be alone and cry, but somehow, I put on a smile and tried to enjoy myself. At the shower, we played all the usual games, and they had a cake with various charms hidden inside. I was one of the lucky ones who found a charm in my piece of cake. Much to my surprise, it was a silver baby rattle. I remember thinking this was either a cruel joke or a sign that everything would turn out okay.

I hoped for the latter.

It had been the longest two weeks of my life, but the appointment day had finally arrived. They did an ultrasound, and much to everyone's surprise, there was a baby and a heartbeat. I burst into tears and so did the ultrasound tech. I had never felt such joy and relief in all my life. We were having a baby, and my due date was February 3, 2004. We were so excited and couldn't wait to tell our family the good news. This would be the first grandchild on my husband's side and the second grandchild on my side of the family.

As the weeks went by, I started to feel the baby moving. It was such a strange feeling at first, but I loved it. It finally felt real, and we looked forward to finding out if we were going to have a boy or a girl. We didn't care what we had, as long as the baby was healthy. We found out we were having a boy. I was so excited. Now I could start shopping for baby clothes and decorate the nursery. I also looked forward to picking out a name for him. I knew the middle name would be William after my grandfather, but we weren't sure about the first name. We had two names and decided to wait until he was born.

My pregnancy continued along well with all the normal aches and pains one would expect. Thankfully, I didn't really have any major issues. During my 35-week checkup, the doctor discovered that the baby hadn't turned yet. They did an ultrasound and discovered that he was a footling breech, meaning he was standing upright with his feet straight down. I was told I would need to have a C-section, and they scheduled an amnio—a test where the doctor removes amniotic fluid and cells from the uterus to learn about the baby's health—at 37 weeks. As long as his lungs were fully developed, they would deliver him the following day. Everything went well, and we were scheduled to have our baby boy on January 15, 2004. At first, I was upset because the 15th was the anniversary of my grandfather's passing, but then I realized it would now be a happy day.

Everything went well, and on January 15, 2004, at 11:23 a.m., we welcomed Evan William Ziemniak into the world. He was so tiny and perfect, weighing six pounds six ounces and 20.5 inches long. We decided to name him "Evan" because that is my husband's middle name, and he looked like an "Evan" to us. We immediately fell in love with him.

Life with a newborn was hectic, to say the least. Evan was very reactive and cried all the time. The only way we could get him to sleep was to hold him in our arms while standing. As soon as we would sit down, he'd start screaming and crying all over again. Matt and I used to take four-hour shifts with Evan so we could get some sleep. He had trouble eating and threw up all the time. He wasn't gaining weight, so we had to start taking him to the doctor's office for weekly weight checks. I started pumping and giving him bottles in addition to nursing him. We couldn't take Evan anywhere because he screamed and cried all the time and he wanted to nurse every hour and a half.

We had friends and family who had babies, but they seemed so much easier than Evan. I knew early on he was unlike other babies. Yes, all babies cry and get fussy at times, but he seemed to cry and fuss about everything *all the time.* He hated dirty diapers but hated having his diaper changed, and he was extremely sensitive to the cold. It was just so difficult to make him happy, and I didn't know what I was doing wrong.

Finally, at his four-month checkup, the doctor diagnosed him with acid reflux and prescribed an antacid. The medicine worked wonders. He started gaining weight, sleeping through the night, and taking regular naps. He slept well but had to be home and in his bed by 7 p.m. every night. Our lives now revolved around his naps and bedtime. I was okay with that, though, because things were finally manageable now that we all could get some sleep.

By this time, I had returned to work full-time as a pharmacist at a nearby hospital, and Matt was in graduate school. We relied on family to help us with Evan at first, but then my husband started working part-time in addition to school, so we needed to find a babysitter. I was concerned about putting Evan in daycare because he was such a handful and required a lot of attention. Thankfully we found a very sweet older couple who were willing to watch him in our home. They quickly became part of the family and were known as Mimi and PopPop. They loved Evan, and Evan loved them.

4

Evan was very attached to me and did not like for me to be away from him. He would scream and cry and hang on to me when I had to leave for work. It broke my heart to have to leave him that way. I wanted so badly to be able to stay home and be with him. I used to cry in the car the whole way to work, and a lot of times, I cried at work too. I enjoyed having a career, but now that I had a baby, I wanted to be home. Unfortunately, it would be a couple of years until I was able to do that.

Evan really was such a sweet and lovable baby. He had this adorable little giggle and sweet smile that always melted my heart. When he was about a year old, he would get so excited when he'd hear me coming home from work, but then when I picked him up, he would start hitting me. It felt as though he was happy to see me but then mad that I had left him. These types of behaviors continued as he got older.

Evan was very smart and started talking early. By the time he was 18 months old, he could speak in complete sentences and people often commented on his use of vocabulary. He continued to be very reactive and rigid about certain things, though. Things had to be his way, or he would throw an absolute fit. I knew some of it was normal toddler behavior, but he always took it to the extreme. He started hitting and biting me more when he did not get his way. We tried time-outs, talking to him, and redirecting him, but nothing worked. I always felt like I must have been doing something wrong and that, in some way, it was my fault he was behaving like that. He didn't do these things to my husband. I was just so frustrated and too embarrassed to talk to anyone about it.

5

It felt like Evan was always at least three steps ahead of me. He was very curious, active, and smart. Sometimes, he was a little too smart for his own good. By the time he was two years old, he was letting air out of my tires and locking me out of the house. He also figured out how to unlock the lock on the back gate and break off the childproof doorknob covers. I would put him in his room for a time-out, and the next thing I knew, he was downstairs telling me how he used his shoe to bang on the doorknob cover and break it off. He also started running away from me around the ages of two to four years old. He would just take off down the street or run through the store, and he was fast. I had a hard time catching him. One time at the store, I turned to grab a cart, and he took off. Before I knew it, he had jumped on one of those motorized carts and ran straight into a display. I was so embarrassed that I grabbed him and left without shopping. It's kind of funny now looking back, but it wasn't at the time. He was just always into something, and I had to be on all the time.

I did a lot of crying and praying in those early years. I prayed that God would keep Evan safe and help me make it through the days. I never thought parenting would be easy, which is why we waited a few years before having him, but honestly, I never knew it would be that hard. I started doubting myself and thinking I wasn't cut out to be a mother.

Evan started preschool at three years old. It was a really nice school, and all of the teachers were really good with him. It was only three hours a day, two days a week. He still didn't like to be away from me. Every single day for school, I had to drag him inside, and the teacher had to pull him off me. It was so upsetting for me, but the teacher said he always calmed down after a few minutes and was fine. He had fun with the other kids, and he always seemed to have friends. Thankfully, by then, I had changed jobs and was only working part-time.

Every Thursday, I picked Evan up from school and took him to Steak 'n Shake for lunch. It was his favorite place to eat, but he would only go through the drive-through, he refused to go inside the restaurant. I thought it was a little odd, but I didn't think too much about it at the time. We had our little routine. We would park, and he would climb in the front seat and eat his lunch. I just thought he really liked getting to sit in the front seat and eat his lunch and maybe that is why he never wanted to go inside.

During the summer of 2007, we were building a new home, and I'd take Evan with me when I went to check how it was progressing. He always brought his toy tools so he could help the "worker men," as he called them. We moved into our new home in September 2007. Evan liked our new house, but he wouldn't let me paint his room, saying everything had to stay the way it was when we moved in. He was not happy at all when I painted the rest of the house. Evan was three going on four years old at the time. Prior to our move, my work schedule changed, and this really upset him. He used to throw temper tantrums, and I remember thinking it didn't seem right that it should upset him so much.

His behavior started worsening, and the hitting and the biting got worse. Evan was always well-behaved at

7

school and there were never any issues. He was only doing these things to me. Time-outs didn't work because he refused to stay in the chair or in his room. I had a hard time getting him to go anywhere with me. He never wanted to leave the house unless it was to go somewhere he wanted to go. I had considered that maybe Evan was on the autism spectrum, but he didn't seem to fit the criteria for it—at least, not the criteria I was aware of. He was rigid and reactive, and he did have to have things a certain way, but he was very social and could carry on a conversation. I thought maybe it was all just a phase, but it continued and worsened.

Chapter 2

Evan started four-year-old preschool in September 2008. It was the same school he went to for three-year-old preschool, but now it was three full days a week. He still did not want to go to school, and every day was a struggle at drop-off. A few times he even gave me a hard time about buckling him in his car seat when I picked him up from school. His behavior started getting worse when we were going places. I would have to fight to get him in the car and then struggle to get him buckled in his car seat, aside from the after school struggle. When Evan was mad about having to go somewhere he didn't want to go, he would throw things at me while I was driving. By then, I was working part-time and working from home. I arranged my schedule so I could take my lunch break at pick-up time. A few times I was late getting back to work because he refused to get in his car seat.

I pretty much stopped taking him anywhere alone. It was just too stressful. He was always well-behaved at school. Evan was a handful and liked to push the limit, but he behaved. His teachers were very good with him and handled him well. He always told them that he missed me, but he did have fun at school with the other children. I knew he was in good hands and was being cared for.

I remember wondering what I was doing wrong. Why was he like this with me and not my husband? I would get looks from strangers at the store, and they would say nasty things to me about my parenting. Even friends and family would say hurtful things. I had no idea why he seemed to overreact over certain situations. I tried my best to be consistent with him, and if I told him he couldn't have something from the store, I stuck with it even when he had a meltdown. I started staying home with him even more. It was much easier than dealing with judgmental stares and comments.

When the weather was nice, I would take him to the playground, and he always had a great time. There used to be an indoor play area at the mall that he loved to go to as well. I would sit and watch him run around having fun and getting his energy out.

I had talked to the pediatrician about some of the issues I was having, and they suggested that I contact a therapist. I finally contacted one when Evan was four going on five.

I remember feeling like a terrible mother for thinking something was wrong with my child. Maybe there was something wrong with me. Whatever it was, I knew I had to do something, and I knew I needed help.

Evan didn't like going to see the therapist and wouldn't talk to her. They did a lot of play therapy, which is commonly done with children. At one point, he told her that she couldn't help him and that no one could help him. He said it felt like he had a helicopter in his head that was spinning really fast.

The therapist said Evan was very intelligent, almost too smart for his own good. She suspected that he had ADHD and possibly anxiety, but he was still a bit too young to be diagnosed. I remember thinking, "Aren't all four- and five-year-old boys wild? And how could he have anxiety at such a young age?" I knew that I got anxious when he acted out, so I thought I was to blame for this type of behavior. I continued taking him to the therapist even though it didn't seem to help. She assured me that, over time, things would start to sink in with him. I was hopeful but had many unanswered questions.

Evan continued to do well in school and seemed to enjoy being around the other children. The kids seemed to really like Evan and wanted to be around him too. He would sometimes act silly to make them laugh. The teacher did notice that he was having a hard time paying attention and sitting still, but he wasn't disruptive.

One day, they did an art project that involved painting the bottoms of their feet. Evan did not want to do it, but after a lot of convincing, the teacher was able to talk him into it. I thought maybe he just didn't like the way it felt, or he didn't want to get dirty. The teacher seemed to imply that Evan was the only student who was hesitant about the art project.

We also discovered that he did not like to be in front of an audience. The school would have them sing songs for the parents for holidays and certain occasions. We noticed that Evan would cover his face with his hands or cover his ears. At the time, we thought maybe he was being shy and didn't want his picture taken or thought it was too loud. I definitely started noticing things and thinking something may be going on, but I just wasn't sure what it was. My nephew had been recently diagnosed with autism, so that did cross my mind, but Evan didn't seem to fit the criteria. I also noticed that Evan was excited to get invited to birthday parties, but when it was time to go, he'd get upset and say he didn't want to go. He could never give me an actual reason as to why he didn't want to go. Just that he didn't want to go. I was always able to talk him into going, though, and once he was there, he'd have a great time. It was getting him there that was the problem.

Evan always seemed to know things that kids his age either didn't know or weren't interested in knowing. He could name all the planets in order at age four. He also liked listening to classical music and could name some of the composers. His favorite song was the "William Tell Overture," and he listened to it all the time. We did notice that he did not like having to write, and his handwriting was messy. He would give us a hard time if he had any worksheets to do at home. Even coloring was a chore for him. I thought that maybe he was just being difficult. He had been in school all day, so he was probably tired and just didn't want to do any work. It never occurred to me that maybe he had some fine motor skill issues.

Evan turned five in January 2009. He was high energy and full of curiosity. He loved to see how things worked, and his interests began to grow. He also started collecting things like rocks, coins, and feathers. If his things were out of place or missing, he would not only notice but get very upset and throw a tantrum. He also did not like for others to touch his things at all. He had trouble sharing his things with other children, but I knew that could be normal. I too was very particular about my things when I was younger, only I was very neat and organized. Evan was messy and not organized at all.

I really enjoyed being Evan's mom and spending so much time with him. He was challenging but also very loving and very sweet. My husband and I had talked about possibly having another child, but I was fine with just one. Evan started telling us that he would like to have a baby sister and that he was going to pray to God and ask him for one. My husband also started saying that he would really like for us to have another baby. At first, I said he was crazy, but then I came around. I thought it would be nice for Evan to have a sibling to grow up with. I said that if it was meant to be then it would happen by a certain date. If not, then it wasn't meant to be, and I would be fine with it.

Just as I was nearing my deadline, I found out I was pregnant and due in December 2009. We waited until after my first doctor's appointment to tell Evan, and then we told our family and friends. He was so excited about becoming a big brother but said he only wanted a sister because a brother would want to play with his toys.

By this time, the school year had come to an end. It was a very exciting time for all of us. A new baby was on the way, and summer break had just started. Shortly after that, Evan broke his leg jumping on a trampoline and spent the next four weeks in a full leg cast. He couldn't put any weight on it, so I had to push him around in a wheelchair. He slowed down a lot, which was welcomed as I was having a lot of nausea with this pregnancy. It wasn't too long before he figured out how to take off in the wheelchair, though. Once, he took off and got on an elevator. The doors closed right as I got to it. I started to panic because I wasn't sure where he would end up and how I would find him. Thankfully there was a nice woman on there who rode the elevator with him back to the floor I was on.

I was becoming more concerned because he just wouldn't listen to me, and I was always afraid he was going to get hurt. It seemed the more I told him not to do something, the more he did it, and vice versa. My husband was concerned too, but Evan was more compliant with him, and he was also faster than me so he could catch up to him quickly. We gave him consequences for not listening like losing TV time or electronics, but he didn't seem to care. I used to pray to God, asking him to protect Evan and keep him safe because I was afraid I couldn't, especially with a new baby on the way.

Evan started kindergarten in September 2009. We decided to keep him at the same school because he did well there, and it was a full day program. Now that he was in kindergarten, he could ride the school bus. There were only two other children on the bus with him, and he seemed to like it. Thankfully, I no longer had to deal with difficult drop-offs.

He continued to do well in school, and he started having occasional homework. It wasn't a lot, but it was a lot for Evan. When I asked him to do it, he would argue and give me a hard time, but eventually he would do it. Still, he spent more time arguing than actually doing the work. His teacher said she would have to keep him on task

14

sometimes, but he cooperated and did his work. They had an evaluation test, and his teacher told us he did well even though he wasn't paying attention. She said had he paid attention, he would have done even better. We knew he was smart, but he just had a hard time paying attention. As I mentioned earlier, the therapist suspected that he might have ADHD, but it had still been a little too soon to diagnose. We would just have to wait and see how the rest of the school year went.

Now that Evan was in school full-time, I was able to get a lot more done on my days off. I could do all my shopping and errands without having to take him with me. This made things a lot less stressful. When he got home from school, I was able to give him my full attention. We still had our evening routines. He loved taking long, warm baths after dinner, and then we would read stories in bed. Evan was still in bed by 7 p.m. every night, which was nice as it gave me some time to relax too. We noticed that Evan did better with routines, so we continued to do what worked best for him.

We started preparing Evan for the arrival of his baby sister. He wanted a baby doll so he could practice holding his sister, and he got to pick out new bedroom furniture. He still didn't want to paint his room, but at least he was happy with his new furniture. And he was still very excited to meet his sister. I decided to have another C-section since I already had one, and we'd be able to arrange babysitters for Evan. We were all very excited, but I was sad to have to be away from Evan for a few days. Plus, I was going to miss his school Christmas program.

Ava Lynn Ziemniak was born on December 16, 2009, and Evan became a big brother. He got to meet her two days later, and we took her home. It was nice because he started Christmas break, so we had time to settle into our new family of four.

Evan did really well with Ava. He loved to hold her, and he tried to console her when she cried. Sometimes he got a little jealous, but for the most part, he was fine. I soon discovered that he did not like to hear her cry, though. He would cover his ears and sometimes hide behind the couch.

Less than one month after Ava was born, Evan turned six. He was really into *Star Wars* and wanted a *Star Wars*-themed party. I don't know how we did it with a newborn, but we did. All the kids dressed up as *Star Wars* characters, and we had a light-up lightsaber cake. It turned out to be a nice party, and Evan and all the kids had a great time.

Things were going well with Ava and Evan. He was in school all day, and I had a lot of alone time with Ava. I already noticed a lot of differences between her and Evan. She was a much easier baby. She had no problems with feedings and didn't cry nearly as much. I was able to take her out and go places with her. In fact, she slept when I took her out. I could still run all my errands and get my shopping done with her while Evan was in school.

We hired a new babysitter when I started back to work. The other couple that had watched Evan was wonderful, but they were getting older, and having a newborn on top of Evan to take care of was a lot. We were

16

very lucky and hired another wonderful couple to take care of Ava and then Evan when he got home from school. Evan already knew them and did well with them, and they were wonderful with the kids. Kim was a retired kindergarten teacher, and we were all so lucky to have her.

Evan continued to have behavioral issues at home, and he was becoming more aggressive with me when things did not go his way. He never hurt his sister, but I would have to lay her in her pack-n-play when he acted out. He would eventually calm down, but it took a while. He was still seeing the therapist, but I still wasn't seeing any improvement. We talked more about having him evaluated for ADHD and anxiety, and she gave me a recommendation for a psychiatrist. My husband and I decided to wait until the summer, and then I would schedule an appointment.

Evan's kindergarten year was coming to an end. It was hard to believe he would be starting first grade at a new school the following year. This was a very emotional time for me. My baby wasn't a baby anymore. For almost six years, he had been my only child. Now he was the big kid, and I had a new baby. I wanted to see him grow up, but it was also very hard to see him move into the next phase of school. I was very comfortable with him being at this little school, and I was nervous about him starting at a new and much bigger school. I would've loved to keep him in that little school forever.

His kindergarten had a little graduation ceremony. The whole time the kids were standing in front, Evan was goofing off and making silly faces. He was the only one acting silly. We just sat there watching and hoping he would stop, but he didn't. My husband and I just exchanged looks—there was nothing we could really do. I wanted to run up on the stage and tell him to stop, but didn't want to draw more attention his way.

After the ceremony, one of his classmate's mothers came up to me and suggested that I have him evaluated for ADHD. I was so embarrassed and upset at the same time. Now others were starting to notice his behavior. I wasn't sure what her intentions were. Was she judging me like others have done, or was she just being a concerned fellow parent and trying to offer me some helpful advice? He was a good kid; he just had tons of energy and acted out occasionally. Once again, I found myself making the difficult decision to call and make an appointment to have Evan evaluated.

Evan was evaluated and diagnosed with ADHD in the summer of 2010 at six years of age. The psychiatrist wanted to start him on a low-dose stimulant called Adderall, but I was concerned. I was worried about starting a six-year-old on that kind of medicine. As a pharmacist, I had dispensed those types of medications many times but it's different when the patient is your own child. Evan was already tiny and thin and did not have much of an appetite, and a side effect of the medicine is decreased appetite. Many patients lose weight and Evan couldn't afford to lose any weight. So, yes, I had many concerns, but I also knew that we needed to try something to help him.

He was going to be starting first grade at a new school, and I was worried about how he would handle it. I knew Evan had some anxiety, although it hadn't been formally diagnosed yet, and he had a hard time adjusting to changes in his routine. We decided that we would start him on the medicine, but we'd wait until closer to the start of the school year.

I reached out to the principal of his new school and shared my concerns with her. I asked if I could bring Evan to meet her and see the school, and she was very accommodating. Evan and I went the following week to meet her at the school. He seemed very excited and was happy to introduce the principal to his baby sister. The school was very nice and was the newest of the elementary schools in the district. She walked us around the school and showed him where the first-grade classrooms were and the cafeteria, gym, pool, library, etc. He seemed very excited. I was hopeful but nervous at the same time. The school was so much bigger than the quaint little school where he had just spent the last three years. We finished the tour and headed home to enjoy the rest of summer and prepare for elementary school.

Chapter 3

In the fall of 2010, Evan started first grade. I was nervous, but somewhat comforted knowing that the school was just a few minutes from our neighborhood. In the mornings, he'd catch the bus with other kids in the neighborhood, and he seemed fine with it. I would walk Evan to the bus stop with Ava in the stroller, and we were always there for him when he got off the bus. We met the bus driver, and he was always very friendly, which made me feel at ease. At first, everything was going well, but after a couple of weeks, we started to have some issues.

Evan had started perseverating, which means obsessing over or fixating on a thought or object—once he was stuck on one thing or idea, it was almost impossible to re-direct him. I remember one time he bugged me for over 45 minutes asking for something. I can't remember what he was asking for, but I just remember thinking I couldn't believe he was still asking for that long after repeatedly being told "no." He just wouldn't give up.

As difficult as it was, I held my ground. I learned to tune him out, and eventually he would give up and move on to something else, but not without putting up a fight. It was the same situation whether we were home or out in public. Once at Target, he insisted that I buy him a toilet plunger. I told him "no," but he insisted. There was no reasoning with him, and he refused to put it back, so I walked away. He chased after me with the plunger in hand still insisting I buy it. Once again, I told him I was not getting it, and he needed to put it back. He was so mad, but he eventually put it down and followed me. To this day I have no idea why he wanted it so badly other than the fact that he liked how it would suction to the ground. It's kind of funny thinking back on it now, but it wasn't funny then.

Even with his medicine, Evan had a really hard time sitting still and concentrating in school. Thankfully, he had a very kind and understanding first grade teacher. She told me he would do things like jumping jacks or hanging off the side of his chair. He wasn't being loud or too disruptive, and she told him that when he was ready, he could sit back down and join the class, which he usually did after a minute or so. When he did this, other kids would tell on him, but she would tell them to mind their own business and pay attention to her.

Academically, he was doing fine, but he still had a hard time with writing and still did not like doing homework (most kids don't enjoy homework, but he *really* didn't like it). He started having daily stomach aches in the mornings before school and saying he was too sick to go. This made our mornings quite difficult. Most of the time my husband had already left for work, so I was alone with a baby and a difficult child. And on the days I worked, I had to get myself ready as well. Thankfully I worked from home, but I still had things to do.

I may have let Evan stay home once or twice before I realized he wasn't really sick ... he seemed to make a miraculous recovery after being told he could stay home. We noticed he only had stomach aches on school mornings or when going somewhere he didn't want to go. He would become very angry and argumentative when I told him he had to go to school, and always said his stomach hurt or he had a headache. He refused to get dressed and get ready for school.

Most mornings were an all-out brawl trying to get him dressed. He would kick, scream, cry and hit me. I had to try to hold him down and dress him. It was awful, and I hated it. I had so many emotions, and it was so very exhausting and upsetting for both of us. It upset me to see him so upset as well. I wanted to keep him home with me, but I also needed a break. Somehow, I still managed to get him ready and on the bus. It always took me a while to calm down afterward because it made me so anxious. I would usually try to straighten up the house a bit and move on to taking care of Ava. There was no time to relax with a little one to take care of.

Then, I started getting calls from the school nurse several days per week. Evan would say he had a headache or a stomachache and ask to see the nurse. She would call and have me talk to him, but that seemed to make matters worse because he would cry and beg me to come pick him up. On the days I worked, I could use that as an excuse not to pick him up, but on the other days, I had to tell him to stay. Eventually, the nurse stopped calling me unless it was something bigger. She would let him sit down for a few minutes, and then send him back to class.

During this time, Evan was also asking to use the restroom frequently. I doubt he always had to go, but it was another excuse to leave class. One day I got a call from his

23

teacher saying she had sent him to see the nurse. He had asked to use the restroom and was gone for several minutes. She sent another boy to go check on him and then he was gone for a while also, so she sent a second boy. They came back and told her Evan was bleeding. She was worried so she ran to get the nurse. It turned out that he had scratched a dry patch of skin, and it started bleeding. Thankfully it wasn't a big deal, but I'm sure it caused a panic when they told her he was bleeding. I started getting used to the daily calls from the nurse and the teacher. I never knew what it was going to be about.

He started perseverating in school around that time. If he saw something he liked, he would ask the teacher for it. It could be a pencil, an eraser, a paper clip, etc. It wasn't usually anything big, and most of the time they gave it to him. He had a way about him. He was charming and so polite that they often couldn't tell him no. His backpack was always full of all kinds of things that he would find on the floor at school. Things like pens, pencils, hair clips, and even broken things. If he saw it, he picked it up and kept it.

At one point, I found a whole bunch of napkins in the storage compartment of his step stool. They were napkins from school. I asked him why he had them, and he said it was because he liked the way they felt. He always had a reason for why he collected and hoarded things and for why he couldn't get rid of things.

Evan started seeing the school guidance counselor to help. He really liked her, and she was very nice and good with him. She started a behavioral plan for him, and he

24

earned prizes for appropriate school behavior. They also set limits on the number of times he could ask for something. It seemed to be working, and things were going well at school. Home, however, was a different story.

I told Evan's therapist about all the issues at school and at home. He was perseverating more, leaving class more, and becoming more argumentative and aggressive at home. It didn't seem that therapy was helping him at all. His psychiatrist increased his medicine dosage, but that didn't seem to help. It got him through the school day, but when he got home, he was very difficult. He was always moving and running around and was in a really bad mood when he got home from school. It was like he used everything he had inside him to keep it together for school, and when he got home, he had nothing left. I thought maybe he was hungry, so I offered him a snack, but that didn't help his mood or behavior. He was becoming more angry, aggressive, and argumentative, more so with me, but with others as well, including my husband.

It seemed that he was becoming increasingly anxious. We noticed that his behavior was worse when my husband was out of town for work. Evan told us that he didn't feel as safe when his dad was not home, and that he didn't like going anywhere because he was afraid of getting in a car accident. He said it wasn't worth the risk to go somewhere he didn't want to go. I asked him why he never got upset about driving to Virginia to visit his cousins, and he said it was because it was worth the risk to be able to see them.

25

Another thing that seemed to bother Evan is that he noticed there were no fire sprinklers in the hallways at school, only in the classrooms. He said he was worried about a fire in the hallway. All of this concerned my husband and me. Evan had never experienced any situation that would cause these types of concerns. We monitored what he watched, so it couldn't have come from anything like that. We were at a loss and had no idea what to do.

His therapist suggested wraparound services—a team of professionals who work with a child at the home, in a family- and community-centered context. I had heard of these types of services because one of Evan's cousins has autism and received wraparound. We were more than willing to try anything that could possibly help Evan. The therapist referred him to be evaluated for the services. If he qualified, he would no longer be able to see his outpatient therapist, but he would receive therapy in our home.

In December of 2010, a psychological evaluation confirmed that he did qualify for the services. The evaluation revealed that Evan had some symptoms of autism, but not enough for a formal diagnosis. Today this is called "autism spectrum disorder," but then it was called "pervasive developmental disorder." The evaluation showed that he had deficits in the identification of his own emotions, and deficits in the use of coping skills to reduce anxiety, rigidness, and anger.

It was hard to take all this in. For so long, I thought I was the cause of the problems and felt like a bad mother, but seeing this evaluation showed that he did have problems. And it wasn't my fault.

Of course, I started wondering if there was something I did during my pregnancy that led to this, but I had been so careful. I didn't even take Tylenol or drink anything other than water. I also felt a sense of relief that we had a better understanding of what was going on and a plan in motion to help him. I was hoping for a miracle and a quick resolution, but that is not what happened. We were at the beginning of a long and difficult journey.

Evan was assigned a behavioral specialist consultant (BSC) and a therapeutic staff support (TSS) worker. The BSC created and oversaw the implementation of a behavioral modification treatment plan for Evan, which we were to follow as well. The TSS worker was supposed to implement behavioral modification interventions.

We met with the BSC, and she developed a plan, but it took a while for the agency to provide a TSS worker. The BSC was very nice, and Evan seemed to take to her, but he was a bit reserved at first. Eventually, we were assigned a TSS worker. I was very happy and hopeful, but it turned out that keeping a TSS worker was challenging. If they showed up at all, they would start to get to know Evan and then quit the agency. Evan did not do well with this at all— it would cause him more anxiety—and it was a big interruption in the treatment plan. He also seemed to be less compliant.

For wraparound to work, you need consistency, and we weren't getting that with the TSS worker(s). Finally, we

27

were assigned a TSS worker who was reliable and consistent. Evan really liked her and enjoyed the one-on-one attention. She did all kinds of things with him like playing outside, playing video games, playing figures, etc. She also worked on trying to get him to do his homework and other non-preferred tasks. He still gave her a hard time but was more compliant with her. I looked forward to the days we had the BSC and TSS worker at our house. They helped me by working with him and giving me a break. Parenting is hard work and parenting a child with any kind of disability is extremely hard work. You always have to be on and ready to go, and that is exhausting. When the BSC and TSS worker were there, it gave me a chance to focus on Ava or get things done around the house.

First grade came to an end in August 2011. Evan did well academically and had A's and B's. I was so very thankful that he had such a kind and understanding teacher and guidance counselor. They really helped him get through first grade. Evan loved being out of school and not having homework, but it could be difficult keeping him busy. If he got bored, he got mischievous.

Some days he seemed to wake up in a bad mood, and those days tended to be more difficult. We always found some type of camp for him, like a video game camp. We also tried swimming lessons, but he really didn't like it because he said the water was too cold. We had a neighborhood pool, but he would only go if the water was warm. From the day he was born, he did not like to be cold. He did enjoy being outside and loved going for nature walks. Our babysitter's husband, who the kids call "Pabo," would take Evan fishing and hiking at a local park. Pabo owned a small airplane and would take Evan to the airport to see all the planes. He really loved hanging out with Pabo, but Evan could also give him a hard time too. We were very lucky to have Pabo and Gramma Kim to help with the kids. I honestly don't know what we would've done without them.

Before we knew it, summer ended, and second grade started. We were thankful to have another good teacher. Evan was still very well-behaved and compliant at school and always had friends. The trips to the nurse and guidance counselor continued, though. He still gave us a hard time about getting dressed and going to school on most days. Even with the wraparound services, we still had problems. Evan was still argumentative and non-compliant at home.

The BSC made all kinds of behavioral charts, but nothing was working. The TSS worker would sometimes go to the store with us, but it was still very stressful. I had been so hopeful that the services would help, but I started feeling defeated.

At Evan's next evaluation, he was approved for a mobile therapist (MT). An MT provides therapy to a child in the home. So now we had three different people coming to the house each week. They really were good and tried their best, but we just couldn't seem to make any progress.

Evan still had a difficult time with handwriting. His teacher contacted me and told me that she had concerns and felt that Evan needed occupational therapy. She said she was going to look into it and get back to me. When she

29

contacted me again, she told me that she kind of got in trouble, though she didn't share why, and was told she shouldn't have suggested to me that he needed occupational therapy. This would be the first of many things the school would refuse to do for Evan.

I appreciated that she shared her concerns with me, and decided to look into outpatient therapy myself. Evan was evaluated and was found to have some fine motor skill issues. This explained the trouble with handwriting and the difficulty he had learning to tie his shoes—he always preferred shoes without laces and didn't want to learn to tie his shoes. In addition to wraparound services, he started outpatient occupational therapy. His therapist was great with him, and he did like her, but he didn't like going. He considered it to be more non-preferred work. Although, there were some things about it that he did like, especially that his therapist always gave him a treat at the end of the session.

Third grade started in the fall of 2012. This is the year things started to become more problematic at school. The work was getting harder, and there was a lot more writing. Evan also started having some issues with kids at school. A lot of the boys were starting to get into sports and played at recess. Evan was not into sports at all. We tried to get him to try baseball or soccer, but he just wasn't interested. He mostly walked around the playground by himself looking for bugs and rocks. Occasionally he said a friend would walk around with him for a bit, but I don't think Evan minded walking around alone. He enjoyed having alone time, especially on days when his mood wasn't good.

He still enjoyed making other kids laugh, too, by doing silly things, and the kids knew this. Sometimes they would tell him to do something, and he'd get in trouble for it. It was never anything big, but I think eventually it started to bother him. One time he said jokingly to a friend "I'm going to kill you," and I got a call from the principal. She seemed to make a big deal out of it, but I explained he was just kidding. I wasn't concerned because I knew my son and knew how he was. Kids had said worse things to him, and no one ever got upset or concerned.

We did have a talk with him and explained that we knew he didn't mean it, but he shouldn't say things like that, especially at school. A lot of times Evan did things that the other kids were doing but they were quiet about it and didn't get in trouble. Evan was never quiet, so he seemed to be the one that got caught. Again, it was never anything big, and I never heard from the school about it. Evan always told us what happened.

Evan's third grade teachers had concerns about him academically. His math teacher told us he was behind in math and his other teacher said he had a hard time focusing in class and following along. His grades were still ok, but he was now starting to get some C's. One of his teachers suggested that he may need evaluated for school services but asked us not to tell anyone they said that because they would get in trouble. I never thought to ask exactly why they would get in trouble. I guess I was just glad that they seemed to care about Evan's well-being.

Evan was still having trouble with handwriting, even though he was having occupational therapy. I started

31

noticing that sometimes Evan would mix up letters and numbers. He would write a *d* instead of a *b* and vice versa. He would also write *15* instead of *51*. His teacher said that it was common for some kids to do that but that usually by third grade they stop. My first thought was that maybe he had dyslexia, but it didn't seem that bad. So, we would just continue to keep an eye on it.

We found out about a new ADHD clinic at a local hospital, so I contacted them to see about getting Evan into the program. It took a while, but he was accepted. The program seemed great—the psychiatrists, who were resident doctors, seemed thorough and knowledgeable. We signed up for the clinic's parenting class as well. It was made for parents with children with ADHD—we were always looking for new ways to help Evan and were more than willing to try anything. The program was valuable; we learned a lot more about why and how parenting an ADHD child is so different than parenting a typical child.

We also learned we had to pick our battles. When Evan would get mad, he would hit and kick. He also would tell me he hated me to try to upset me. I could just ignore him when he said mean things, but I couldn't ignore the hitting and kicking. For some families, if their child said they hated them, it would be a big deal. For me, that was nothing compared to the other problems. The program also offered cognitive behavior therapy (CBT), so we signed Evan up for that. CBT is based on the idea that how we think, feel, and behave all interact together. It helps kids (and adults) to understand how their thoughts determine their behavior. Evan started the program but unfortunately, the psychiatrist who was working with him

32

was involved in a serious car accident and was unable to continue teaching the program.

We started looking into having Evan tested for special education services at school. The school has so many weeks to complete the evaluation from the time of the initial request. While we waited for the school, we decided to have Evan evaluated by an outside psychologist. At this point, it appeared to me that the school was trying to avoid doing anything for Evan, despite the teachers' concerns. We had a meeting with school personnel, including pupil services to discuss our concerns and why we wanted them to evaluate Evan. One person sat at the table looking at their watch, and you could tell they were annoyed to be at this meeting. Another school member seemed condescending to us—we felt like they were trying to make us believe there was no reason for Evan to be evaluated.

I remember feeling so upset about this meeting—my husband was too. Their actions and words made us feel that they would rather be anywhere else other than sitting in that meeting listening to our concerns.

They eventually did the evaluation—the results were different than the one we had done with the outside psychologist. The school evaluation stated that they didn't really see any issues with Evan and that he appeared to be able to pay attention. They didn't see any issues with his math abilities, but he had been seeing the math support teacher. We also had been having issues reading Evan's handwriting, and he was forgetting to bring some work home. The school provided the students with an agenda book for homework assignments. I could hardly read his handwriting, and when I asked Evan what it said, he couldn't read it either.

The evaluation we had done listed some recommendations that they felt would help Evan. Some of the recommendations were for the teacher to double-check his agenda to make sure it was legible and that he had everything he needed for homework. They also suggested that Evan have decreased writing assignments and decreased math assignments in addition to more time to take math tests and quizzes if needed. We requested that the school provide Evan with an individualized education program (IEP) and to follow the above recommendations.

But they did not want to do an IEP, saying that he didn't need it; however, they said they would do a 504 plan and follow the recommendations provided by the outside psychologist. (A 504 plan is meant to provide accommodations for children with qualifying disabilities to ensure academic success.) We also requested occupational therapy in school, but they stated that because he had already been receiving outpatient occupational therapy, they did not want to provide it in school. We were satisfied that they agreed to the accommodations, but I'm not sure they would have agreed to any of this had we not had our own evaluation done. I couldn't believe how much we had to fight to get help for our son. It was exhausting and upsetting.

Little did we know things would only get worse.

Third grade finally came to an end. I was relieved that we had a 504 plan in place for the following year and was hopeful that it would help. We definitely had more issues in third grade, and it seemed as though Evan was having trouble with friends. Evan had different interests than most of the kids. The other boys were into sports and Evan was into history and antiques. He was also into video games and playing Minecraft, though, so he had that in common with the other kids. A new family moved onto our street that year, and they had two boys. One was Evan's age, and the brother was two years older. They all got along well and played together often. I was so happy that he had some kids his age to play with.

During the summer, Evan went to a Minecraft camp, which was a video game camp. He seemed to enjoy it once he got there but it was difficult to get him to go. He would have rather stayed home and played video games. At least at the camp, he was around other kids, and they got to design their own games. We also signed him up for a back handspring camp since he loved doing flips and was good at it. He really loved parkour, so when we found out that they offered a boys' parkour class, we signed him up. That was actually the only activity he ever stuck with. (In case you don't know, parkour is a non-competitive sport that involves jumping, rolling, running, climbing, and vaulting to get on, over, or around obstacles ... I always called it "ninja training"!)

Before we knew it, summer was over, and school was starting. Evan started fourth grade in the fall of 2013. Ava started three-year-old preschool at the same school Evan attended for preschool and kindergarten. For the first time in a few years, I was going to have time to myself. I was no longer working, so I had a lot more time to spend with the kids, which was great. As in previous years, the school year started off okay, but that didn't last long.

Evan's teacher wasn't always following his 504 plan, and it felt like I was constantly calling her about it. I got the feeling that she did not think Evan needed it and did not want to follow it. She was supposed to make sure he wrote all his assignments in his agenda, make sure it was legible, and make sure he packed all the books he needed in his backpack. I think she only started following it because she got tired of hearing from me. Once I heard her sigh over the phone as if she was annoyed to hear from me. She used to tell me that Evan was fine, and she had a lot of experience with kids with ADHD. Perhaps she did have experience with kids with ADHD, but I reminded her that all kids were different, and I knew my child best. Evan used to say she was not the right kind of teacher for him, and I agreed.

The teacher had something called a strike system for homework. She had each student's name on the front board, and next to their name she had three strikes. If a student forgot to do a homework assignment or didn't finish their homework, she would have them walk up to the board in front of the class and remove a strike. After three strikes in a quarter, she would give them detention. At the end of each quarter, she would have a strike party for the students who still had all three strikes. They would have snacks and listen to music while the other students who were missing strikes were made to sit in the hall during the party. Evan always said he would never get to go to a party

36

because, no matter how hard he tried, he always forgot something. He even said it wasn't even worth trying. Both Evan and I were very upset about this. I can understand that kids need to do their homework, but it's not okay to publicly shame them and make them feel bad about themselves. Evan did his homework, but occasionally he would forget something. I told him I would always be proud of him, as long as he was doing his best.

One time she removed a strike for not doing an assignment, but she didn't make sure the assignment was written in his agenda. I called her and told her he was not losing a strike when she did not follow his 504 plan. She did not sound happy at all, but she knew I was right and that she could get in trouble for not following it. I also told her about how awful and shameful her strike system was. I tried to explain to her how this could be upsetting to a child like Evan and that it would hurt them, not help them. She basically just said she had been doing this for years and she was not planning to stop. I came right out and told her she was mean, and she said she had been told that before. I couldn't believe she just didn't care.

Evan played the trumpet in fourth grade and was pretty good at it, considering he couldn't read the music. I asked him how he played it, and he told me that he watched the other kids and saw where to put his fingers. He figured out on his own how to play part of a song he liked on the trumpet. I never would have been able to do something like that. He ended up quitting because he said it was too much work and he didn't want to play in the concerts in front of a crowd of people. Evan had taken karate in the past and was good at it too but ended up quitting. I think he just got bored with things after a while. Parkour was the only thing he stuck with, and I was glad he finally found something he liked.

Fourth grade finally came to an end, and I think we were all happy about that. I always looked forward to not having homework to fight about, but it was also hard to plan activities that both kids wanted to do. Ava wanted to go swimming, but Evan wanted to stay home. And the older Ava got, the more they fought. It almost seemed like she knew when he was having a bad day, so she would keep pushing his buttons. Sometimes Evan would be in a bad mood for no apparent reason and wanted to be left alone. These were the days she just wouldn't leave him alone, and he'd end up hitting her. Yet, she'd keep going back.

Thankfully for the most part they got along, and they really did love each other. Evan was very protective of her, and Ava adored him. We did have a lot of happy times together and a lot of dance parties in the family room. We also welcomed a new family member, a black and white kitten. Evan had been begging us for a cat for so long, and we finally gave in. He named her Kit Kat after his favorite candy bar. It was an exciting time for the kids.

That summer we took a family vacation to Savannah, Ga. I love history and old homes, and so did Evan. We all had a really good time, for the most part. Ava was only four years old at the time and didn't share our love of history, but we still did a lot of things that she enjoyed too. We finished out the summer with a couple of camps and short trips. Before we knew it, summer was over, and Evan was heading to fifth grade.

Evan was ten, and as I reflect back on our lives to this point, I thought it was important to mention this: The summers were enjoyable, but they could also be difficult when I was trying to keep kids happy and busy. If it were up to Evan, he would've just stayed inside playing video games ... but that's not the best way to spend the summer. If you have a child with special needs, I recommend finding at least one summer camp or activity your child enjoys— not only is it important for them to be around other children, but also to give yourself a break. We need to take care of ourselves to take care of our children. Most days felt like being on a battlefield dealing with all the challenges that come with special needs children. Even just having an hour to yourself to sit and relax can do a lot of good for your mental health.

Chapter 4

Evan started fifth grade in the fall of 2014. It was hard to believe he was entering his last year at the elementary school. At the same time, Ava was starting four-year-old preschool at the same school she'd been in during the previous year. What a difference between Evan and Ava. Unlike Evan, Ava loved school and looked forward to going. She never cried when I dropped her off. Sometimes I didn't know what to do with myself, but I quickly adjusted to having both kids in school all day. I was relaxed about Ava, but always on edge about Evan.

It didn't take long before we started having issues. Evan became increasingly anxious about going to school and became even more aggressive with me. He did not want to go to school and tried anything he could to get out of going. He would hit, kick, bite, scream, cry, and throw things at me. Most mornings he barely made it on the bus, and then it was time to take Ava to school. One morning Evan seemed to be in a pretty good mood. He had gotten dressed, eaten breakfast, and was ready for school. He had some time before the bus came and asked if he could ride his bike for a bit. I told him that was fine and continued getting Ava ready for school. I walked outside to get him on the bus, and he was nowhere to be found. I started calling him, but he didn't answer. His bus came and went and no Evan. I started to panic, and a couple of my neighbors helped me look for him. We walked down the street calling his name. We finally found him hiding with his bike in a little wooded area off of the street. I was so angry and upset but relieved that we found him. I still made him go to school, and he was not happy about it.

The calls from the school nurse continued. Once she told me I was a saint. I didn't think I was a saint. I was just a mother who loved her son and would've done anything for him. That's what a mother does. I would've gone to hell and back—and at times it sure felt like I had.

At some point, he became obsessed with something called an "e-hookah," which is like an e-cigarette or vape pen. We do not smoke, so I was surprised he even knew anything about it. I think a neighbor had one and Evan thought it looked cool. He was convinced that he needed one because it would make him feel calm. We explained that they are not for kids, and they are not safe.

Evan wouldn't stop talking about it, and he started looking them up on his iPad. He kept arguing with us and trying to convince us that they are safe. He even asked a doctor about them and was not happy when he told Evan they are not safe. Evan decided he would send a letter to the company stating why he felt they should change the age limit and allow children to use them. He actually wrote them a letter. It was kind of impressive how persistent he was and how he argued his case. We always said he would've made a great lawyer.

The obsession with the e-hookah continued and worsened. It was all he talked about—at home, at school ... even with strangers. It was becoming extremely overwhelming and concerning. He became angry and aggressive when told we would not buy one for him. We talked to the school guidance counselor and principal about it, and they told him that it was not appropriate to talk about it in school. They were surprised to hear about all the issues we were having with him at home because they said he was always so well-behaved in school. They also told me that if I ever had any issues getting him to school that we could call them, and they would pick him up.

Things were becoming increasingly difficult at home. One evening in particular was very bad. Evan was out of control screaming and yelling and throwing things. This time my husband was home. Evan had gone up to his bedroom and locked his door. I followed him and used a pin to unlock the door. As I opened the door, I saw Evan with his bedroom window open, about to climb out. I was so upset. He claimed that he was trying to climb out onto the sunroom roof. From the back, his room was three stories up. I explained that he could've fallen out and died, and he said he didn't care. His behavior was so concerning that we decided to take him to the psychiatric hospital. I was scared out of my mind.

We called Pabo and Kim, and they immediately came to get Ava for us. That hospital was the scariest place I had ever been. It was awful. I didn't feel like we belonged there, and I couldn't wait to go home. The whole time we were there, Evan was swearing and telling us that he did not want to be there. He saw that the room had a camera, and he was not happy that someone could see him. He was like a completely different kid. It was like Evan had left his body and someone else took over. The doctor came in and talked to us and to Evan. I think they just wanted to make sure that Evan was not a threat to himself or to anyone else. He sent us home and told us to follow up with the psychiatrist.

I'm not sure what I expected from our hospital visit, but I thought maybe the doctor would've been a bit concerned. I realize they see lots of patients in more urgent situations, but this was urgent to us. This was the child that we loved with all our hearts, and he needed help. I felt like we were losing Evan and no one else cared, not even the mental health professionals.

One day, I received an unexpected package. When I opened it, I discovered it was an e-hookah. Apparently, Evan had gone on my phone and ordered one from the Amazon app. I couldn't believe he had done that. I was in a hurry at the time, so I hid it inside a pitcher in the dining room. Obviously, my husband and I had a talk with Evan about the whole thing, and he was very upset. He still didn't understand why we wouldn't let him have it.

Shortly after that, my husband went out of town for work. Evan was always more difficult to handle when Matt was out of town. At one point, Evan had told us that his dad was stronger than me and could protect him if anyone were to break into the house. He did not feel safe when I was home alone with them. We had never had a break-in, and we lived in a safe neighborhood. In fact, the police station was just down the road from our neighborhood. We also had an alarm system and assured Evan that we were safe.

It was a Friday after school, and I was home alone with the kids. Evan started on me again about the e-hookah, and he was getting more and more agitated. I could see that he was starting to escalate, and I was trying to talk him down, but it wasn't working. We were outside, and he picked something up and threw it at me. For the life of me, I can't remember what it was. He grabbed his bike and took off down the street. I was calling for him to come back but he kept going. I had Ava with me so I couldn't take off after him. He was never allowed off our street and I was worried he would get hit by a car.

I didn't know what else to do so in a panic I called the non-emergency number for the police. I explained to them that my son had ADHD and anxiety and that I was concerned for his safety.

There were at least two police cars at my house within a few minutes. One of the officers drove off to look for him while the other one stayed with me to get information. I was mortified because some of the neighbors came outside to see what was happening. After a few minutes, I saw the police car slowly driving up our street while Evan was walking along beside him with his bike. The officers were very nice, and I couldn't believe how quickly they responded.

I was worried that Evan would give the officers a hard time but thankfully he didn't, and they were so kind and patient with him. They asked him why he took off and he told them it was because I would not let him have the e-hookah. They had never heard of it before, so Evan started telling them all about it. One of the officers actually got

45

inside his vehicle so he could look it up on his tablet. They told him that he should listen to me and not give me a hard time. We went back inside, and Evan was well-behaved for the rest of the evening.

I was very impressed with how well the officers handled Evan. He did not like being told what to do, so he felt defensive around authority. Evan thought of himself as an adult and therefore felt like he needed to defend his maturity. I was so relieved that they took a gentle approach with Evan and were so patient and attentive.

The following week was another tough one with my husband still out of town. On Friday morning before school, Evan refused to go. He was still upset that we would not let him have an e-hookah. He started throwing things, hitting me, opening kitchen cabinets, and dumping his food on the floor. No matter what I did, I could not get him to calm down. I just stood there crying and watched him tear up the house. I realized that, if I tried to intervene, it only made his behavior worse.

I was at my wit's end, and I remembered that the principal and guidance counselor had told me that if I ever needed anything to call them and they would come over. I didn't want to have to call them, but I was so worried about Evan, and I felt I didn't have a choice. He had already missed the bus, and I knew I needed help because there was no way I could have handled him being home with me.

When they walked in my front door, they saw Evan and the mess and then just looked at each other in total disbelief. They had never seen Evan like this. He was

46

always well-behaved, so they were shocked and concerned. They talked with him and calmed him down. He really liked the guidance counselor, and she was so good with him. They were trying to convince him to go to school with them, and at first, he refused to go but then the principal told him that if he went, he would not have to do any schoolwork that day. He finally agreed to go with them.

I felt a huge relief that they were able to get him to go with them. I don't know what I would've done without their help. Later that day, the principal sent me an email saying how concerned she was for me and that she was afraid Evan would hurt me someday. She also mentioned that Evan argued with her and the guidance counselor about how he thought the e-hookah was okay for him. I really feel that, on that day, we hit rock bottom. We needed to do something else for him, but I just didn't know what else there was to do. I felt hopeless and helpless.

I told Evan's psychiatrist everything that had been going on. I told him that my husband and I were at a loss with what else we could do. We were worried that Evan was going to hurt himself accidentally. When he got upset, he lost total control of his emotions. It was like someone flipped a switch and Evan was gone. I could look into his eyes, and it seemed like he was looking right through me. We also explained how Evan's obsession with the e-hookah was taking over all our lives. It was all he talked about. I really believe that Evan thought the e-hookah would somehow make him feel better, and the fact that we would not let him have something he thought would help him was upsetting to him. Therefore, he acted out and got aggressive.

The doctor recommended a partial hospital program. It was an outpatient program that focused on intense therapy. For two to four weeks, Evan would go to the outpatient program instead of going to school. They would still do some schoolwork, but most of the day would be therapy. I was nervous about him going there because I wasn't sure what to expect or how Evan would handle it, but I knew we needed to try something. We had tried so many other things over the years and we were running out of options. Evan was not happy to hear that we were going to send him to the partial program, but we explained that we were only trying to help him.

I contacted the school to let them know about the partial program and hoped they could offer some guidance, but unfortunately, they had no experience with it. They said that Evan was their first student, and they weren't sure how to handle it. The guidance counselor was more than willing to help in any way she could and offered to speak to the social worker at the partial program.

Evan was admitted to the program at the beginning of October. At first, I started taking him and picking him, up but then after the first week, the school provided transportation. As expected, Evan gave us a really hard time, and one of the counselors would have to come out to get him, but he cooperated with them. He also gave me a hard time getting on the bus. The driver was very nice and sometimes brought her little girl with her. I felt bad that he would act out in front of them, but the driver said once they left, he was always very polite and well-behaved. She said he was very sweet to her daughter and sat with her on the bus. I was so relieved to hear that.

48

I had so many mixed emotions about Evan going to the partial program. I was hopeful but afraid. What if this didn't help? The next step was an inpatient program, and the thought of that really scared me. Evan told us about the other kids who were in the program with him. Some of them came from abusive homes and had some medical issues as a result of the abuse. It was so heartbreaking, and I was concerned about how it would affect Evan. In a way maybe it was good for him to see that. Maybe he would appreciate what we were trying to do for him. We love him so much and just wanted what was best for him. We wanted him to be happy.

I was also concerned that he would fall behind in his schoolwork. The teacher at the partial program suggested that I ask the school for some worksheets, and she would do them with him. I reached out to his teacher, but she told me I would need to speak to the guidance counselor while Evan was in the partial program. So, I contacted the guidance counselor, and she was able to get the worksheets from his teacher.

Evan was doing well for the most part. It took a while, but eventually he talked less about the e-hookahs. While he was there, one of their psychiatrists met with him and made some changes to his medications. I figured we'd try it, and if it didn't work, his psychiatrist could always change them back. I talked to the social worker, and they decided to keep Evan in the program for the full four weeks. He would be back to school just in time for the school Halloween party and parade. He was very excited about that and looking forward to seeing his friends.

I contacted the school to let them know and to also find out how they would transition him back to school. I was worried about what the other kids would say to him and where he would say he had been. His classmates had already been asking where he was and when he was coming back. The teacher told them that he had gone to a different school but would be coming back at the end of October.

On the last day of the program, we had a discharge meeting with the partial program social worker and teacher and Evan's principal, teacher, and guidance counselor. Evan had been given an education evaluation while he was there, and it showed that he had fallen behind in math. This had been brought up in previous years, but school personnel always downplayed it, saying he was fine. Once again, they downplayed it, saying that they use different testing and according to their test he was fine.

We requested that his math and writing homework be reduced to help decrease the issues we were having at home. Immediately his teacher became defensive, and claimed that she did not give too much homework. I explained that it may not be too much homework in general, but for Evan, it was too much. The partial program teacher spoke up, agreeing with the recommendation. The principal said they would make the changes to Evan's 504 plan.

I could tell that they really didn't want to make the changes, but they knew we weren't backing down, so they went along with it. We talked about how Evan would be transitioned back to the classroom and what would be said to his classmates. Everyone agreed that it would be best to tell them that he had gone to a different school for tutoring and to leave it at that. They would let the students know he would be back on Monday.

I was looking forward to having Evan back at school and hoping for the best, but I was very anxious. I wasn't sure what the kids would say to him about where he had been for the past four weeks. And I was also concerned about the teacher. She seemed defensive at the meeting, and I could sense that she didn't agree with the changes to his 504 plan. I really wanted the best for Evan. He had been through so much, and I just wanted him to be happy and do well.

Evan was excited to go back to school and looked forward to seeing his friends. He said that the kids were happy to have him back and, of course, were asking him where he was. He told them he went to a special school for a while, and I guess he just left it at that. Evan had started sniffling and clearing his throat a lot, which we figured out was a side effect from the new medication. It was a tic, which he couldn't help. Unfortunately this led to him making loud noises in class, and some of the kids started commenting. Some of them were saying really mean things to him, which upset him. I couldn't believe this was happening now.

We had just been through hell the first month of school, which led to the partial hospital program, and now we had to deal with this. I had already scheduled a follow-up appointment with Evan's psychiatrist to discuss the medication changes made by the other psychiatrist. I was definitely going to see about discontinuing the new medication.

I contacted Evan's teacher and the guidance counselor about the issue. Some of the kids were telling Evan to go blow his nose and that he was being annoying. The guidance counselor said she planned to have a discussion with his class while he was at his psychiatrist appointment. She told them that Evan couldn't control it and that telling him to stop would be like asking someone not to sneeze. She also told them that they would not tolerate anyone picking on him. The psychiatrist changed his medications back, and eventually the tic went away.

The school psychologist made the changes to Evan's 504 plan as discussed at the partial program discharge meeting. We were going to schedule a meeting to discuss the changes, and I wanted to have an educational advocate there to support us, since I didn't feel that the school was taking Evan's needs seriously. An educational advocate is someone who can support families and provide information about the rights of children with disabilities. There are paid advocates and there are free advocates. Both will help you, but the free advocates are very busy.

I tried very hard to schedule the meeting around the advocate's availability, but unfortunately the school could not accommodate her schedule. I was able to send her a copy of Evan's updated 504 plan so she could at least look over it. I was disappointed that she couldn't attend the meeting, and I wondered if the school purposely did not accommodate her schedule. I didn't understand why the school seemed to not want to provide special accommodations for Evan. He had the diagnoses to support the need for help, but they always said he needed help.

There was an employee at the school who thought Evan needed the help, but they were unable to say anything because they thought they might get in trouble. This was the same issue with other school personnel in the past. Everyone was afraid of getting in trouble while my son suffered. It wasn't right, so I kept fighting.

I had an appointment scheduled for Evan to have an educational evaluation done by a private psychologist. I had to pay out of pocket for it, but it was worth it. I had also done some research and found out about something called "dysgraphia." Dysgraphia is a learning disability that causes difficulties in writing. Everything I read sounded exactly like Evan's handwriting issues. He had spatial issues, difficulty staying in the lines, and his handwriting was almost illegible. I asked to have him tested for this as well at the evaluation.

Just as I expected, Evan did have a form of dysgraphia, but he did not have any other learning disabilities. In addition to the other accommodations he already had in his 504 plan, we asked the school to provide occupational therapy. They did not think it was necessary, but we insisted so they agreed. The school occupational therapist provided him with some worksheets to help him, along with raised line paper to help him stay in the lines. He was given more time to complete tests if necessary and was not to be graded on his handwriting. He was also

53

allowed to take verbal tests instead of written tests when needed.

To be honest, the worksheets and the raised line paper didn't really help, but at least he had the other accommodations, which did help a bit. I couldn't help but feel that the school was only doing the bare minimum and that was only because I pushed for the modifications. I never understood why it seemed they didn't want to do anything for him. Was it the extra time and effort, or was it the money? If all the therapists and psychologists that I took Evan to could see he was in need of the extra accommodations, then why could he not get the help?

By now, the school year was almost over. They started sending home information about middle school, and they had planned a day to take the fifth graders to tour the school. I was getting nervous at the thought of him going to middle school. We had such a difficult time at the beginning of the school year, and I was worried about how he would handle being in a new school that was even bigger.

Around this time, Evan started having some issues with another student. This particular student was causing problems for other students as well, and Evan was very upset. I contacted the teacher, the principal, and the guidance counselor to make them aware of the issue. The guidance counselor told me that she was aware of the issues with this particular student as other students had told her they were being picked on as well. She told me that she would follow up with the principal and let me know what was going to be done, but we never heard back.

Evan had enough one day and went to the office asking to see the principal. He told her that he was tired of how this student was treating him and others and demanded that they do something about it. The principal finally called me and told me that she spoke to the student's mother. The problem was that this student's mother was involved in the school. So, nothing ever happened to the student, and they were never punished for picking on my son and the other students. I requested that this student not be in any of Evan's classes at the middle school.

I told Evan that I was proud of him for speaking up for himself and for the other students. It was also very brave of him to do it. A lot of adults have trouble doing this, and here he was, just an 11-year-old little boy, standing up for what is right. He wasn't the least bit afraid. He just did what he felt was right. I could see that all of our hard work was paying off.

It was finally time for the end-of-fifth-grade party. I volunteered to help with the party and to make favors. Evan was so happy that I was chaperoning the party. I met them at the school and rode the bus with the kids to Latitude 360. It was a big arcade, and they were also going to have a dance party.

Evan had such a good time dancing and showing off all his cool dance moves. He did head spins, back spins, and flips. I took a video of him dancing and sent it to the guidance counselor. We were so happy to see him having the time of his life dancing with his friends. We went back to school and passed out their favors, along with t-shirts that said class of 2022 which is the year they would graduate from high school.

The last week of school had arrived, and Evan was looking forward to the end-of-year video. The school started this tradition the previous year. They picked a song and then filmed a video with all the students and staff. The song for the video was Taylor Swift's "Shake It Off," and Evan was asked to do some of his dance moves. He was so excited because Taylor Swift happened to be his favorite singer at the time. I was elated to see him so happy. We had such a difficult year, and it seemed like things were finally getting better.

We had such a good summer, probably the best we ever had. Evan and I went antiquing a few times. We finally found our thing together. He loved finding treasures, and he was good at bargaining. People were always so amazed by him! Not many little kids enjoy antiquing with their moms. We also found a blacksmith camp for him. It was a bit of a drive, but it was worth it. He really enjoyed it there, and we still have the things he made. We also took a family vacation to the Outer Banks with family and had a really great time. Over the summer, we had family-based therapy. It is similar to wraparound services, but it involves the whole family. Ava really enjoyed it because she got to participate, and we did a lot of crafting activities. Overall, I think it went well and was good for us. Evan seemed to be in a much better place over the summer. We were always willing to try anything that could possibly help.

As summer went on, I started worrying more and more about middle school. Evan seemed excited about it, but I just couldn't stop crying. I didn't know why at the time, but I just had a bad feeling.

There were two different orientations that summer. The first was for students with 504s and IEPs, and the second one was for all students. He got to take a tour of the school and see where his locker was. I even took a picture of him in his locker for fun. We found another psychology office that came highly recommended, and we had Evan evaluated one last time before sixth grade. This time he was diagnosed with extremely high-functioning autism. We had been told years before that it was possible that Evan would eventually be diagnosed as he got older.

I contacted the school to alert them and see if there was anything else they could do for him. As usual, I didn't feel like the school wanted to do anything more for him. I was told that a diagnosis of autism wouldn't change anything and wouldn't make him eligible for an IEP or any additional accommodations.

I was beyond frustrated at this point. I knew my son needed more than the school was willing to offer him. Because I was persistent, the head of pupil services finally agreed to put Evan in a math class that had a math support teacher in addition to the regular math teacher. They also agreed to provide Evan with a laptop so he could type out assignments instead of writing. We then arranged to have a meeting to discuss the changes to his 504 plan.

Before we knew it, summer had come to an end. On the last day of summer vacation, I had a pizza party for Evan and Ava and some of their neighborhood friends. It was a great way to end the summer. Evan was heading to sixth grade, and Ava was heading to kindergarten at the elementary school.

Chapter 5

Evan started sixth grade in the fall of 2015. He seemed very excited about it and liked the fact that he would be changing classrooms for each class. Within the very first week, though, I had to contact the principal because Evan's 504 wasn't completely being followed. I was told that his teachers had not been made aware that he had a 504 plan. I was very frustrated by this and was becoming more concerned. We'd had a hard enough time in elementary school getting a single teacher to follow the plan, and now he had several teachers. The plan was eventually distributed to each of his teachers, and I hoped that would make a difference.

At the same time, Ava started kindergarten at the elementary school. She adjusted quickly to the new school and seemed excited to be there and be with her friends—but with Evan, it was completely the opposite. We really wanted to see Evan happy as well and came up with something we knew would lift his spirits.

Evan had wanted to go to Gettysburg for quite some time, so we took him that Labor Day weekend. He had always been fascinated with war history, especially the Civil War. He told us once that he had been in a war before and that he flew a plane. We thought he was just making it up, but he seemed adamant about it. Looking back, it makes me wonder. I did always call him an "old soul."

We toured the battlefield and went through some old homes and antique shops. We found a shop with Morgan dollars, which Evan had always wanted, and we got him two. One was from the late 1890s and the other was from the early 1900s. He was so ecstatic about the coins that it made the guy selling them to us a little emotional. I'm so happy that we got to take him to Gettysburg, and to have those family memories. We all loved that trip.

As the weeks went by, Evan started having problems at school. One student started giving him a hard time, making rude comments and throwing papers at him in the cafeteria during lunch. A cafeteria worker noticed and reported the bully to the principal, and the student got lunch detention as punishment. Then things got worse. The bully was just a miserable child and enjoyed picking on others. He told Evan that he was an atheist and that there would be no consequences for his actions. He even said that he enjoyed tormenting others. Evan told this boy that, although you cannot see God, there is a God, and you need to have faith. And he told him that there *are* consequences. He also told this boy that he could not just go around being mean to people.

The whole situation made me livid. Why couldn't these kids just leave Evan alone? He never did anything to anyone, and he certainly didn't deserve to be mistreated. I immediately contacted the school and spoke with the principal and guidance counselor about the issue. The principal spoke to Evan and the other kid about what was going on, and while they were talking, Evan told the boy that he understood if he had problems because he had

60

them too. Then Evan said that he'd be his friend if he needed one. The principal called me and told me she had talked to them, and she told me what Evan said to the boy and how touched she was. She also said the boy got tears in his eyes. I hoped that this would solve the problem, but I should've known better.

Things at home were finally going better, but things at school were getting worse. The boy continued to cause problems for Evan and now other kids were also mistreating him. Evan no longer gave me any issues about going to school, though. In fact, the mornings were great. I'd get up early with him every day, and we'd have the best conversations at the kitchen table while he had his breakfast. My husband and daughter were still in bed, so it was just Evan and me. I had discovered the previous year that if Evan's clothes were warm, he would hurry up and put them on. So, every morning from then on, I put his clothes in the dryer for ten minutes. I couldn't believe it worked and wished I had thought of this years ago.

Occasionally, Evan would ask to stay home, but he no longer got upset when I said "no." If he was sick, then of course I let him stay home. I no longer received calls from the school nurse, but Evan still made his way to the nurse's office several days a week. He also made several trips to the counselor's office, but they weren't always available. He would come home from school and tell me that he really needed to talk to them, but they were hardly ever there. If he had been crying, the secretary would let him sit in the chair for a few minutes to calm down and then send him back to class. I always asked him if someone did something or said something to upset him but, he just said he felt stressed in class and needed to take a break. He usually told me some of what was going on, but later, I found out there were a lot of things that he never told us.

Evan did well with his classes—his favorites were science and social studies. He still gave us a hard time about doing homework, but I could usually work with him, and he'd get it done eventually. He still struggled with math like he always had and fought with me the most over math homework. His teacher decreased the amount of math homework he had to do, but it was still too much for Evan. His perfect amount of homework would've been none at all, but he seemed to do better if my husband did math with him. His two friends that lived down the street always did their homework as soon as they got home from school and weren't allowed to play until 4:00. I tried to get him to go along with that, but it hardly ever worked. He wanted to play video games to pass the time until they could play, and usually, he would make his way down there before 4:00. Their mother always told me Evan was so polite and would ask if she could make an exception and let them play earlier, but she always told him to come back later. And he always made his way back down there at exactly 4:00.

They were such nice boys, and they got along so well—I was glad to see him happy. We had been through so much over the years, and that's all I wanted for him. The boys had a younger sister who often came over to play with Ava. Having all of the kids playing together and getting along well brought me a lot of joy.

Evan had a harder time in English language arts—mostly because of the writing, but also because it was two full periods back-to-back, as was Math. Sitting for that long was just too much for him, so he would ask to leave. He would ask to see the nurse or the guidance counselor or to use the restroom—anything to get out of the classroom. The guidance counselor made a card for Evan to place on his desk instead of asking the teacher to leave the classroom. The card had multiple phrases on it, such as "I need a break" or "I'm feeling overwhelmed"—which was, in my opinion, a little too childlike for a sixth grader.

Kids were already picking on him, and this just gave them more fuel—when he would ask to leave the class, they made rude comments. Evan told me the kids would say things like "Oh, do you need a break? Do you need to go see the counselor again?" If the teachers heard them, they would tell the kids to knock it off, but plenty of things were still said and done that went unnoticed by the teachers. Kids have a sneaky way about them. I told the guidance counselor that the break card and the other fidget toys they gave him were just making things worse. They were making Evan even more of a target, and everything just kept adding to Evan's anxiety.

One day, the kid who had been giving Evan the most trouble told him that his biggest wish was to "lock Evan inside the school and set it on fire." When Evan told his teacher, she told him to stay beside her for the remainder of the class and stay away from that kid. I couldn't believe it when he told me. I immediately called the school (like I always did) and was assured that they would talk to the kid yet again. This kid had just made a threatening statement to Evan, and they were not taking it seriously. We asked to have another meeting and this time we wanted the boy's parents to be there.

We were told, however, that the parents were not willing to meet. And then we were told that this child was in a situation that no child should ever have to be in. I said that I felt bad for this child if he was in any way suffering, however my child did not deserve to suffer as a result. My son had multiple diagnoses too. He had been through hell the previous year, and he definitely did not deserve to be tormented by this troubled kid.

Through it all, Evan continued to offer him his friendship and show him kindness. One day Evan came home and told me that the boy told him he had tried to hang himself. I immediately contacted the school so they could contact his parents. I told Evan that I was proud of him for telling me so the boy could get the proper help. Evan was always looking out for other kids. He didn't like to see anyone suffer because he knew how it felt and he didn't want anyone to feel bad. I didn't realize the significance of this at the time.

Another kid confided in Evan, telling him that his dad drank a lot and would sometimes hit him and his brother. He said his dad broke his iPad over his head and then showed him the bump on his head. Evan told him that it wasn't normal to do that and that his parents never hit him. I contacted the school to let them know this as well but never heard anything else about it. It seemed there were many troubled children, and Evan was trying to help them—but no one seemed to be helping Evan.

Evan was still seeing a therapist weekly and a psychiatrist monthly. Things were going okay with the therapy itself, but Evan would often resist leaving the house for those appointments. Other times we'd make it there, but he'd take his time going into the office when the therapist was ready. He still had to give a little struggle, but eventually he'd go. There was a snack machine in the lobby, so I'd tell him he could get something if he cooperated. Mostly he just liked to check the change return for leftover coins.

One time he asked the therapist if he could borrow a magazine, and she told him he could. The cover said something like "How do others see me?" I asked him why he wanted the magazine, and he said because everyone always looked at him like he was weird, and he wanted to know why. My heart broke into a million pieces for him. I hated that he was struggling at school with the other children. I was relieved that things at home were finally going well, but things at school continued to worsen. I was constantly contacting the school for some reason or another. It seemed like we'd tackle one issue, and then another one would pop up. All these things just kept adding to Evan's anxiety.

The bully that gave Evan the most grief rode on the same bus as Evan every other week, and he bothered everyone else on the bus too. At first, he was saying annoying things or banging on the back of the seat. Evan would sit with his friends, who somehow would find a way to just ignore him, but Evan couldn't. This kid would purposely sit near Evan, knowing how much he bothered

Evan, and he kept doing it. As he had told him before, it gave him pleasure to torment others.

One day, Evan came home from school in a terrible mood. I asked him what was wrong. He showed me his hand and said the bully had stabbed him in the hand several times with a pencil. You could see the indentations in his skin from the pencil tip. I was livid.

Evan said the bully had been sitting in the seat behind him and his friend, and he was banging on the window beside Evan's head. They kept telling him to stop, but he wouldn't. Finally, Evan had enough, and he put his hand on the window to stop him. That's when the bully took a pencil and started stabbing Evan in the hand. He got up out of his seat, grabbed the bully by the arm, and told him to knock it off. Of course, that's what the bus driver saw so she assumed Evan was causing the problem. I immediately contacted the school and left a message for the principal. I managed to calm Evan down and told him I would take care of it and not to worry. He no longer got aggressive with me, and I certainly didn't want this child to upset him and make things worse at home. We were finally in a good place, and I wanted to keep it that way.

I spoke with the principal the following day, and she said she would talk to the bus driver and make sure she kept the bully away from Evan. I decided that I would walk down to the bus stop after school and talk to the driver myself. I knew that Evan and his friends were the last kids on the, bus so I wouldn't be delaying her.

66

The boys got off the bus, and I introduced myself and told her that I had just wanted to make sure the principal contacted her. I never approached the bus doors or even touched them. I just stood on the grass with the boys. She immediately got nasty with me, saying that she already knew what was going on and that my son was not an angel. I was taken aback by her tone. I had tried to be as polite as possible in my attempt to ensure things were taken care of. I told her that I knew my son was not an angel but that he was not the one stabbing someone with a pencil. Rudely, she said that I was holding her up, closed the bus doors, and took off.

We all just stood there looking at each other in disbelief over what had happened. Evan was so protective of me and was extremely upset about how the driver had spoken to me. I was upset and shaken up too but tried to remain calm for the boys. We walked to his friends' house to speak to their mom about it. She was not aware of any of the issues, as the boys never told her. I remember her telling them she couldn't believe they just let him do those things and didn't tell anyone. When we got home, I left a message for the principal and called the bus garage. The woman I spoke to was also very rude, claiming that the bus driver would've never spoken to me like that and, if she did, then it must've been my fault.

I was so angry. All I had been trying to do was protect my son and had been nothing but nice to the bus driver. I contacted the transportation secretary to let her know what was going on. As soon as I told her the bully's name, she told me she had seen his name come across her desk several times. I found out from others that he was causing trouble with other children on the bus he rode the opposite weeks. And yet no one had done anything about any of it. The boy just continued to ride the bus and torment the kids.

The following Monday, I spoke to the principal about the bus driver, who said that it was no surprise that she was rude, as she was not known to be a friendly person. I had no idea that things were about to get worse. When Evan got home from school, he told me that the bus driver gave him an assigned seat. He had to sit in the first seat alone and was not allowed to sit with his friends. The bully, however, could still sit anywhere he wanted. Yet again, I was floored. How does that make any sense? My son was not the troublemaker, yet he was being punished.

The principal and I went back and forth over the situation, and eventually the bus driver gave the bully an assigned seat also. It wasn't right that Evan had to sit alone since he wasn't the one causing problems, and yet no one would do anything about it. The transportation secretary offered to put Evan on a different bus, but he didn't want to be without his friends. I didn't blame him one bit. I also offered to drive Evan and his friends to school, but he said he'd just stick with the bus.

Christmas break was right around the corner. I had gotten chocolates for Evan's teacher and the bus driver. I told Evan it was the right thing to do. He refused to take the bus driver chocolates saying that bad behavior didn't deserve rewards. I couldn't argue with him. He was right. We had said that same thing to him a million times. If it held true for him, then it should hold true for everyone.

What I didn't know was that Evan told her that there were chocolates for her, but he refused to give them to her. He had also told her that it was okay to have a bad day once in a while but that she can't be mean to them every day. He really had no filter and would just tell it like it was. It didn't matter if you were a kid or an adult. If Evan thought it, you were going to hear it. I think it was part of being on the spectrum. We tried explaining that sometimes things can be hurtful, but he didn't always get it.

We had a nice Christmas break. I think by this time, Evan knew we were Santa, but he went along with it for Ava. He had winked at me when talking about his Christmas list, so I took that to mean he knew. Evan had some interesting things on his Christmas list. He was into old electronics and video game consoles. He even asked for a record player with an eight-track, which he received. What sixth grader wanted an eight-track player, let alone even knew what one was? That was Evan. He just had a different way about him and was an old soul. I really loved that about him. He was my special boy. Ava had just turned six before Christmas and Evan would be turning 12 in a couple of weeks. Being sandwiched between two birthdays, Christmas was a busy time for us, but I always liked all the hustle and bustle—it made everything that much more special.

When the kids went back to school, the bus saga continued. Evan had asked the bus driver when he could sit in the regular seats again—she said that as long as he was in middle school on her bus, he would have an assigned seat. This, of course, upset him. I spoke to the principal on Evan's birthday and told her that we had had enough. I said that starting the following week Evan was to no longer have an assigned seat. She agreed with me and told me she would tell the bus driver. Evan's friends were over to join in our family birthday celebration, and they were in the basement playing video games. I went down and told them the good news. They were all so happy. A little while later, Evan came upstairs saying he didn't feel well and wanted to go to bed, but he wanted his friends to stay so they could play video games. They weren't allowed to play video games often, and he didn't want them to have to go home early and miss out on game time. I told him that was fine with me. He was always thinking of others even when he was sick. The poor kid slept right through the family birthday celebration and didn't even eat his cake.

Evan went to school the following week and sat with his friends on the bus since the principal said she was going to talk to the bus driver. Apparently, that never happened because the bus driver screamed at him and told him to get in his assigned seat. He tried telling her that the principal said he didn't have to sit there anymore, and she told him she didn't care. He came home upset and crying saying that he was so sick and tired of everything and that he just didn't want to live anymore. That was it. I called the principal and told her what Evan said. I demanded that she take care of this once and for all or I was going to contact the Superintendent and show up at the bus garage.

Needless to say, the next morning there was no longer an assigned seat.

During this time there was another situation going on at the middle school with the eighth graders. The school had an activity called a kindness workshop, where the students would sit in a circle, and were then asked personal questions. If they answered "yes" to the questions, they were to walk into the center of the circle. The problem is that the questions were about topics such as sexual orientation, the criminal history of their parents, and so on. Obviously, this caused a huge problem with parents and students, in part because the activity would give more ammunition to bullies. (It was later confirmed that this activity was created for young adults and should have never been used on middle school students.) So, Evan's issues with the bus driver and bully were put aside because the school was too busy dealing with that issue. We were glad that it was all behind us, but my poor son had suffered unnecessarily for over a month.

Evan had turned 12 on January 15, 2016, and had a birthday party with his friends later in the month at the Coin Operated Hall of Fame, an old school arcade with tons of pinball machines and other vintage games. It was like stepping back into an 80's arcade, and Evan loved it there. He was so excited for his party and had lots of his friends there. He even wore sunglasses and driving gloves. He was so funny and was such a free spirit.

Ava enjoyed the party too. She adored her big brother and loved doing all the things he loved. She had been playing video games and watching movies with him from the time she was just a tiny toddler. Evan adored her too, even though she could be an "annoying" little sister at times and knew how to push his buttons. He was great with her and very protective. They fought just like any other siblings, but they had a very strong bond and loved each other so much. You can see the love in every single picture I ever took of them together. I was the luckiest mother to have my beautiful babies.

Evan had many interests over the years, but a new interest for him was ghost hunting. I'm not sure how he got into it, but he had asked for a ghost-hunting device for his birthday. I bought him a cheap one because I didn't really believe in it at the time but figured it couldn't hurt him. It was supposed to detect changes in electrical energy. One day while we were in his room, he said to me "Mommy, do you know why lights flicker when ghosts are around?" I said "no" and asked him why. He said, "because they interfere with electrical energy, causing the lights to flicker." He was also into Nikola Tesla and had been working on devising a plan to make his own Tesla Coil. He even had drawings in a notebook. He was very determined and had asked Pabo to help him make one.

Around this time, he had a science project to do. The kids had to come up with a sentence using the abbreviations for the periodic table of elements. Evan told his teacher that he wanted his to be about Nikola Tesla. She was so impressed that he even knew who he was and told him that, if he could do it, she would give him extra credit. He was determined and did it. He came up with "Nikola Tesla is one very famous person," which is Ni+K+O+La Te+S+La   I+S   O+Ne   V+Er+Y   F+Am+O+U+S P+Er+S+O+N. He impressed all of us. Evan was a smart kid when put his mind to it. If it was something he liked, there was no stopping him. He had even made it on the honor roll that year. We were incredibly proud of him.

Things continued to get worse at school. The bully had been picking on Evan in the mornings before school, and other kids weren't being nice to him either. No one stood up for him. I started getting more emails from Evan's teachers saying that he started leaving class more often. He would say he didn't feel well and go to the nurse's office. Sometimes he would fall asleep in the nurse's office, and they would just let him sleep because they felt so bad for him.

Things were worse than we thought. I received a call from one of the guidance counselors saying that Evan was presenting with the most amount of anxiety she had ever seen in a child, and nothing she was doing was helping him. She was at a loss and said she was going to consult one of the school psychologists. I had been telling them all along that his anxiety was getting worse and school was the trigger. They kept telling me he was fine because he was well-behaved in school and was getting good grades. At one point, I was told that they were going to have the bully switch his last two periods so he wouldn't be in the same class as Evan. That never happened, and when I asked why it didn't happen, I was told because the boy didn't want to switch classes. I wasn't sure why the child was being given the option, when he had been the one causing the problems.

We scheduled another big school meeting. His teachers talked about how they couldn't keep him in class and how he was always saying his stomach was upset and he didn't feel well. I could see that they were concerned, and so was the guidance counselor. I asked them to give Evan a modified schedule. The classes he was struggling in the most were math and English language arts (ELA) because they were each two periods in a row. I wanted them to allow Evan to only have one class period for math and one class period for ELA.

At that point, I didn't care about his grades. I was just concerned for his mental health. He was doing so well at home, but he was struggling at school. I knew other kids had accommodations for anxiety, and I wanted them to do it for Evan. They refused, claiming he didn't need it. At one point, the psychologist looked at me across the table and asked if Evan was even in therapy. I said yes, he was in therapy, and they were helping him, but the school needed to help him also. As far as I was concerned, school was the trigger, and they needed to do more.

Evan's therapist and psychiatrist offered to meet with the school so they could all come up with a plan of action for Evan, but the school refused, claiming that there was no need to meet. The school decided that, instead of making things easier for Evan, they were going to get tough with him. To me, this sounded both arrogant and incompetent. They were going to take away all his breaks and provide his teachers with the things Evan used as reasons to leave, like a water bottle or Chapstick, so he couldn't find excuses to leave class.

I felt my heart drop and my throat tighten. I could barely speak without crying. I told them this was a bad idea, that things at home were finally good, and this was going to ruin everything we had worked so hard for. My husband was scheduled to go out of town the following week, so they agreed to hold off until he came back because things were always worse when he wasn't home. I was just disgusted by their lack of support and on top of it all, felt defeated and hopeless.

They eventually met with Evan to discuss the new plan. They told me he cried but went along with it. Things didn't get worse at home, and I was surprised. He really didn't talk much about school—in fact, he mentioned that the bully was being nice to him. I warned him and told him to be careful because I just didn't trust this kid. He seemed really happy that this kid was talking to him now. He had tried so hard all year to get this kid to be accepting of him, but I never understood why. I was just happy that Evan was happy, and there were only a couple of months left of school. Soon Easter break would be here, and summer would be here before we knew it.

The last day of school before Easter break was March 23, 2016. It was a Wednesday, and the kids only had a half day of school, so I spent the morning cleaning and doing laundry. We always had the holidays at our house so I was in a rush to get as much done that day as I could. I took a quick break and checked out Facebook. I happened upon an article about a family who lost their 12-year-old son. He had been doing something called "the choking game," and he accidentally hanged himself. I had never heard of such a thing, but I immediately thought to myself that I would talk to Evan about it when he got home. I had also received an email from one of the school psychologists saying that she was proud of Evan for having done such a great job at staying in class. I was going to mention that to him as well.

Before I knew it, Evan was home, upset about an argument he had earlier in the day with a couple of his friends. He was such a sensitive child who easily took things to heart. I sat down on the couch with him, and we talked. I even tried calling one of the boys' moms. I left a message asking her to call me back. I told Evan not to worry about it and that we would handle it.

We had a nice long conversation about what we were going to do over Easter break. We had plans to go to a carpet skate park and to see a new movie that just came out. He was excited about Kit Kat's second birthday, which was coming up in two days. He had planned to order Angelia's pizza and get vanilla ice cream with the chocolate caramel cups in it. As a special treat, he was going to let Kit Kat have a lick of the ice cream. I mentioned to him that the school psychologist emailed me to say he was doing well. He said, "Well, they won't let me leave so I really don't have a choice." I told him I was proud of him. He mentioned that he had plans to go down the street to play with the boys, but first, he wanted to go take a warm bath. He had started doing that as a way to relax.

He was up there for a while and then finally came downstairs. He pointed out to me that he was wearing a watch and said he had forgotten he had it. He said he was heading down the street. I reminded him that he had parkour that evening, and then he took off out the front door. By now, Ava had come home from school and came upstairs with me while I dried my hair. Evan came in the front door and yelled up the stairs. He said the boys weren't home, and he was confused because they made plans on the bus to get together. He said something about

76

going out to the garage to look for something, but I didn't hear what he said. I didn't think anything of it, and then I heard him go outside.

Ava and I came downstairs, and she saw her friends outside playing and wanted to join them. It was a beautiful, warm, sunny March day, and everyone was outside. I watched Ava run up two houses to her friend's house, and then I looked around for Evan. He didn't answer me, so I just assumed he had run back down the street looking for the boys. I went back inside to finish up some things. I went back outside a while later and called for him, again and again. He didn't answer. I walked up to where Ava was and asked her if she had seen Evan. She said he was just out back running around in our yard and then took off into the little wooded area behind the houses. There was a tree stand back there where the kids often played.

Just then, my neighbor came outside, and we chatted for about 15 minutes. I told her that I couldn't find Evan and I was starting to get a little concerned. Mostly, I was annoyed. I figured he was just down the street and hadn't told me. On the way back to my house I stopped at the edge of the neighbor's yard and could see the tree stand, but Evan wasn't there. I called for him again but still got no answer. I decided I would run in the house and throw a pizza in the oven and then walk back to the tree stand. I never went back there because I was always afraid of snakes and creepy things, so I was annoyed that I had to now.

The trees hadn't started blooming yet, so I could see clearly through the woods. As, I walked in behind our swing set, calling his name, I found him.

He was kneeling next to a tree. I could see his eyes were open and looking straight ahead. I said, "There you are! I've been calling you. Where have you been?" He wasn't answering me, and I started to panic as I walked faster to get to him. My heart was pounding, and my body felt heavy. He wasn't far away from me, but it felt like it was taking me forever to get to him. It was like I was moving in slow motion. There were prickly thorns on the shrubs, and I could feel them scratching me as I hurried toward him. I started yelling, "Evan, answer me! Why aren't you answering me? Answer me!"

I was frantic by now and as I got up to him, I noticed the rope around his neck, and I saw the deep red mark. His eyes were open, his mouth was slightly open, and his head was leaning slightly to the side, against the tree. I lost it, and immediately started screaming, "No, No, Oh my God no! Evan, what did you do?" I reached down to pick him up, but he felt so heavy, and he slipped out of my arms. I reached down again, and this time I picked him up. I put my knee up against the tree and held him on it. I could feel that his back was warm, but his face was cold and there was a tiny blue streak on his cheek. I remembered that I had my cell phone in my pocket, and I called 911. The whole time I was screaming for help. A recording came on saying for me to hold for an operator. I was panicking and on hold.

78

Finally, someone answered, and I kept screaming, "Oh my God, my son is hanging from a tree!" I don't know why I said that because he wasn't hanging from a tree, he was kneeling. He kept telling me to calm down, and I kept trying to say our address. I was getting angry because I thought I was speaking clearly, and I didn't want him to waste time. I kept saying that the police station was just down the street. Also, I didn't understand why I needed to tell him my address because I thought my address should just pop up, but I forgot I was on my cell phone.

I suddenly remembered that the kids had been outside playing and realized that they might hear me screaming and come back there. I didn't want them to see Evan, so I quieted myself down while the 911 operator was trying to get me to do CPR. I tried but couldn't. I didn't think I could lay him down on the ground, so I just begged them to get there quickly. Evan started to make a gurgling sound and I thought he was trying to breathe.

I had all these thoughts running through my mind, and I had no idea what he had done. My first thought was suicide because what else could it have been? I knew Evan had been struggling, but he was never suicidal. I admit that I did worry about that for when he got older but not now. Not a 12-year-old child. I kept thinking that we'd get him help. He'd have to be hospitalized and go through therapy. Maybe he would have a little brain damage because of the lack of oxygen, but we'd do whatever we had to do to help him.

I just wanted my son.

Someone was trying to call me while I was on the phone with 911. It was my neighbor. I couldn't answer the phone, but I just hoped the kids hadn't heard me. Finally, I heard sirens in the distance. I looked down the woods and I noticed a neighbor walking up to me. At the same time, an EMT and an officer were walking down to me. The EMT froze when he saw us and took a step back like he was in shock. My neighbor had a knife and asked if he should cut the rope. The EMT snapped into action. I remember saying, "please don't cut him," and put my hand between the rope and Evan's neck. They cut the rope and the EMT grabbed Evan out of my arms.

I turned around and fell to the ground, screaming and crying. My face was soaking wet, and covered in leaves. They were stuck in my hair and on my face. By then, the other EMTs and police had arrived. I remember the detective and another officer—it might have been the lieutenant—stood on either side of me and pulled me up from the ground. I remember seeing the other EMTs and hearing one of them ask for the defibrillators. They said they left them in the ambulance and one of them took off to get them. I remember thinking *why the hell wouldn't you bring them*? They were wasting precious time.

A lot of what happened is like a blur or like a movie playing. I was there, but I didn't feel like it was really happening. They walked me to my back porch steps, and I sat down. They were trying to get me inside, but I wouldn't go. I tried calling my husband, but he didn't answer. I then called my aunt who lived close by. Thankfully, my uncle came home early from work that day, so he rushed right over. I then called Pabo and Kim and told them to come and get Ava. They finally were able to get me inside the house after I made my phone calls.

The police asked me question after question, and I just kept standing there trying to answer them. I kept trying to go outside to find Evan, and each time they would stop me. They said that all my neighbors were outside, and it was best if I stayed inside. My uncle had left in the ambulance with Evan, and I didn't even realize it at the time. Thankfully my friend Sabrina came running up and was there with me. The officer kept trying to get me to go with him to the hospital, but I was in complete shock. I started cleaning the kitchen and putting away the food. I then ran upstairs and grabbed Evan's pillow because I knew he would want it when he woke up. It was a small pillow that he had had since he was 15 months old. He called it his "ABC pillow" because of the alphabet pillowcase.

I said I would only go to the hospital if Sabrina took me. The police officer kept saying he'd take me because he could get me there faster, but I refused. I don't know why I wouldn't go with him. I guess I didn't feel comfortable with him because I didn't know him. I knew Sabrina, and she was a comfort to me. We walked outside and down the sidewalk to her car.

Neighbors were lined up and down the sidewalk as well as several police cars and unmarked cars. The drive to the hospital was excruciating. My stomach was in knots, and I just remember leaning forward and staring at the dashboard. I tried calling my sister-in-law, Katie, but she didn't answer. It's probably a good thing she didn't answer.

Sabrina was calling her husband and asking him to call our priest. I remember her telling me to pray, but I couldn't. I just kept thinking, *it's too late.*

I then got a call from my uncle asking where I was and seeing when I'd be getting to the hospital. I knew it was bad. I just knew. He told me that the doctors were doing everything they could, but his heart wasn't starting. I knew he was gone. Being in healthcare, I knew enough to know your brain can't go that long without oxygen. My uncle said they were waiting for me and my husband to get there and then they would have to stop. I don't even know what I was thinking in that moment—I just knew I had to get to the hospital.

There was traffic, and we weren't moving. I could see the hospital and wanted to jump out of the car and run there, but Sabrina talked me out of it. I ran inside, and they showed me to a room where my uncle was waiting. The doctor came out to talk to me. By then my husband was there. His friend drove him from work.

I remember that the doctor looked young, and he told us that they had tried everything they could, but his heart monitor never even bleeped once. They asked my husband and me if we wanted to go into the ER room where they were working on Evan to see him one last time before they stopped working on him. I said I didn't want to because I was afraid to see him with all those tubes and wires, and I didn't want to see them doing CPR. They continued to do it until we gave them permission to stop. My husband went to see him at that point, but I just couldn't. I didn't want to remember him that way. It was

82

bad enough I had found him, but at least he looked fine. After they stopped working on him and disconnected everything, they brought him into the room with us, and we were able to spend time with him before they took him to the morgue.

There was my sweet boy. He was gone. I just couldn't believe it.

I went to him and touched him. He felt cold this time, and I could see that his little ears had purple blotches. The sheet was pulled up over his mouth because they had to leave the tube in him, and I could see a tiny bit of blood.

I just stood over him touching him and crying. I asked for a chair, sat down, and laid my head down with his pillow. One of the nurses brought in a cart with water and snacks. My mother, my brother and his wife, my uncle, Sabrina, and my husband's friend were all there. I just remember telling my mom that they couldn't save him.

Our priest was unable to make it, but another priest came in and gave Evan his last rites. Matt asked the priest what would happen to Evan if he did in fact die by suicide. The priest told him that God knows what's in his heart and that's all that mattered. I suppose that brought us a little comfort.

I don't even know how long we all sat in there. They told us we could stay as long as we wanted. When we were leaving, one of the nurses was crying, and she told me that she prayed so hard over Evan. She kept telling me he was so beautiful. I kissed Evan before I left, and touched his foot as I walked away. I told the nurse to please take care of him, and we left the hospital without our beautiful boy.

We had to contact a funeral home. I had no idea what to do or who to call. This was all too much. We just lost our son, and now we had to find a funeral home. Sabrina suggested one, so we called them. Now we had to tell Ava. Pabo and Kim brought her home. They hadn't told her anything. She knew Evan got hurt and had to go to the hospital, but that's all she knew.

I sat her on my lap, and we told her that Evan had an accident, he couldn't be saved, and now he was in heaven with God. She was only six years old at the time and didn't really understand what was going on. She asked what happened to him, so we told her he had been playing on the tree stand and fell off and hurt his head. I didn't know what else to tell her. I didn't want to tell her what had really happened. Honestly, we didn't know what *had* really happened, but we knew people were saying he killed himself.

It was all over Facebook before we even got home. There were pictures of him captioned with *RIP Evan*. That night, Ava slept in bed with me, and my husband slept in Evan's room. I didn't sleep at all. I was so sick to my stomach and shaking. I just lay in bed crying all night.

Suddenly, I remembered the article I read earlier in the day about the boy who died playing the choking game. I searched for it and read it again. It sounded very similar to what happened to Evan. I started thinking that maybe that

84

was what he did, but I just had no idea what to think. I was in shock and in the worst pain I had ever felt in my life.

The next week was a blur. Our house was full of family and friends who came to support us and help us with Ava. People sent flowers and brought us food and gifts for Ava. I couldn't eat but at least we had food for our guests. The phone never stopped ringing. I received calls from many of Evan's teachers and school personnel, and many of them stopped by the house to see us.

The funeral director came over to our house to make arrangements. I had no idea what to do. Easter was in a couple of days, so he suggested waiting until the following Monday to start the viewings. He asked us where we wanted to bury him, and I panicked. I couldn't bury him. What if we moved away? I couldn't leave him. We are Catholic, so I thought we couldn't cremate him, but I just couldn't bury him. The funeral director said we could still do a viewing and have a Catholic Mass and then instead of going to a cemetery, they would take him to be cremated. The thought made me sick, but at least I'd be able to keep his ashes with me.

We had to pick out an outfit for Evan. I had bought him a nice light green and blue plaid button-down shirt for Easter, so I decided to have him wear that with a pair of his favorite jeans. I laid the outfit on his bed, and I later found Kit Kat sleeping on it. I asked the funeral director to keep the cat hair on his shirt because I knew Evan would've wanted that. He picked off some of the cat hairs and tucked them in Evan's shirt pocket. The funeral director was so wonderful to us. He and his wife had lost an infant child, so

85

they were all too familiar with the pain. He did everything he could to help us get through the viewing and the funeral.

So many people came to the viewings—the police, teachers, bus drivers, Evan's parkour instructors, Ava's dance teachers, and nurses from the hospital. It was so very touching. I couldn't believe how many kids came to see my sweet boy. It broke my heart even more to see them crying. I just couldn't believe my Evan was in that coffin. He looked like he was sleeping. I so badly wanted to hug him and kiss him, but I hated that he felt cold and hard.

Somehow, I got through those days, and now we had to get through the funeral. I picked out all the songs I wanted to be played. One of his classmates was an altar boy, and a teacher sang "Ave Maria."

I sat in the pew and just stared at Evan's coffin. I had Ava to keep me distracted. She was wearing a beautiful light green dress that matched Evan's shirt. Their outfits were meant to be worn for Easter, but instead, they were worn for a funeral.

After the mass, I walked down the aisle behind Evan. All of a sudden, I felt faint, and my legs started to give out. Someone from the school noticed and came running out and caught me. I hadn't eaten more than a few bites of food over the previous week, and I was weak and exhausted. My stomach was in knots, and my heart ached. I hadn't slept more than four hours a night. I had never experienced this type of pain and fatigue before. I just kept thinking that I'd never see my beautiful boy again, and I had no idea how I was going to survive.

The funeral director had people handing out blue balloons to everyone as they walked outside the funeral home. The police had stopped traffic and were all standing outside. People got out of their cars and stood with their heads down. The funeral director also surprised us with a dove release, and they played Billy Joel's "Piano Man," Evan's favorite song at the time. It was so beautiful (if you can really say a funeral is beautiful); they put so much effort and thought into it. We appreciated everything everyone had done for us. So much.

After the luncheon, we went back home. I was in a fog and don't remember much—but I'll never forget the cardinals. I looked out the back windows and saw that my yard was filled with them. I had never seen anything so beautiful before. I wish I would've thought to take a picture, but I wasn't in a good state of mind at the time. A friend of ours who also saw the cardinals said that it was our family coming to let us know that they had Evan with them. I really hoped so. I hoped they had him and were taking care of him.

Chapter 6

The days were long and hard, and the nights were even worse. Everyone went home and continued with their lives, but my life stopped the day my son's ended.

I don't know how I made it through those early days. I just put all my effort into trying to make sure Ava was taken care of. My husband went back to work, and Ava went back to school. I stayed home alone with Kit Kat, sleeping most of the days away unless I had a guest.

Early on, people often stopped by to check on me and spend time with me. It helped to have the company and support. I had extreme anxiety and was unable to leave my house. I remember feeling like my heart was going to jump out of my chest, and I felt like I was suffocating. My stomach was in constant knots, and I wanted to crawl out of my skin and get as far away from myself as I possibly could. I was feeling things that I had never felt before, and for the first time in my life, I felt dependent on others. It was terrifying for me. Having the company was a welcome distraction, and I appreciated the visits.

People invited me to go for walks or to go out to lunch, and I appreciated that they thought of me, but they had no idea how hard it was for me. I felt like people were staring at me when I would go out places. I know they really weren't, but that's how it felt. I would have panic attacks in the stores when I walked by something I used to

89

buy for Evan. I would go to reach for it out of instinct but then quickly remember I no longer needed to buy him anything. Then I'd start crying right there in the middle of the store. It was so embarrassing, and I hated feeling so weak and fragile.

People told me to let them know if there was anything they could do for me, but the truth is that I had no idea what I needed. I knew I needed my son, but no one could bring him back.

I couldn't help but think about what had happened to Evan. The coroner ruled his death as suicide, but it just didn't make sense. I knew he had struggles, but he loved us, and he loved his cat. He wouldn't have left us on purpose, but I just had no idea what he had done.

A few days after we lost Evan, the school sent out an email to the entire school district stating that our son died by suicide and that suicide can be the result of a mental health illness. They never consulted us or asked for our permission.

I was so upset and contacted the school right away, but they just kept trying to justify their reasons for doing it. Apparently, they only meant to send it to the middle school parents but somehow it was sent to the entire district. In addition, a separate email was sent to the parents of the elementary school he had attended. A few people contacted the school to say that they shouldn't have sent that email especially the part about suicide being the result of a mental health illness. The school revised the email, taking out the mental health illness part, but the damage was

90

already done. Everyone had already received the initial email. I felt violated, and I felt that my son was violated.

Thinking back now, I remember the day that I got the call from the coroner's office, when they told me that they were ruling Evan's death as suicide. I wanted to say, "No, what if I don't think that is what happened?" but instead I said nothing. I was too weak and too numb to fight it at the time.

As time went on, I did a lot of research. I recalled the choking game article I saw the morning of Evan's passing, and that is what prompted me to investigate further. I researched the choking game and suicide. I was trying to look for anything to prove Evan's death was an accident. I found out from the EMT who lived in our neighborhood that Evan's trachea had not been broken, which meant his death was not caused by a drop hang. Most suicides are drop hangs, meaning the person jumps down from something. That is not what happened with Evan. He had been kneeling and leaning forward. He was found in the same position as other kids who had died from the choking game.

I started asking the parents of Evan's friends to ask their kids if they had heard of "the choking game" or "pass-out challenge." Every single one of them said they had never heard of it, but I wasn't convinced that was true—I thought maybe they were too afraid to admit they had.

Evan's electronics had been forensically checked by the Pittsburgh Police Department, and they found nothing about the choking game or suicide. All that meant is that he never looked anything up on his iPad, but that didn't mean that someone else hadn't told him about the choking game. I started having a feeling that the bully had something to do with all of this. I remembered that he had told Evan he tried to hang himself but *what if he was talking about the choking game*? I also remembered Evan told me a couple of weeks before he died that the bully was finally being nice to him. I just didn't trust this kid. I couldn't explain it, but I knew he was involved in some way.

Through my research, I discovered that there was such a thing as a "psychological autopsy." During a psychological autopsy, information gathered about the deceased from family members, friends, and healthcare professionals is used to further determine if the death was a suicide or an accident. I knew that this was something I needed to have done.

I contacted the coroner's office and spoke to the coroner who had done Evan's autopsy. I told him that I didn't feel that Evan's death was a suicide but instead an accident related to the choking game. I also told him that I wanted to have a psychological autopsy done.

He told me that in the initial report someone said my son was suicidal. I asked who had said such a thing, and he told me it was in the police report. No one knew who said it or how it ended up on the report, though. I told him that was absolutely not true, and I wanted to talk to him about the events and conversations with Evan on the day he died.

He agreed to talk to me, and I proceeded to tell him everything that happened that day. He said that he agreed with what I said: Evan was making plans, and that did not sound like suicide. He asked me to write a letter explaining everything we had talked about, and he would present it to the board and have Evan's death changed to accidental.

Several weeks went by before I finally heard back about changing Evan's cause of death. I had called a few times but was told they were still reviewing it. Eventually, I spoke to an assistant who told me the board met and decided to change the cause of death to "undetermined." I told him that was not what the coroner and I talked about, and I was not going to accept anything other than "accidental." I spoke with the coroner again, and he said he agreed that it was accidental, but the board did not agree—in fact, they didn't want to change it all. He told me that I could speak to the lead coroner, so I immediately asked to speak with him.

He was not as convinced as the other coroner. He told me that they almost never change a cause of death from "suicide" to "accidental." At best, they would agree to "undetermined." I told him that was not acceptable because Evan's death was not undetermined, it was accidental.

He tried arguing with me by saying that Evan had ADHD, to which I said, "Lots of people have ADHD, and they don't die by suicide." Then he stated that between all of his staff they had over 100 years of experience. I quickly told him that may be, but I had 12 years of experience with my son, and all they had was a few hours with his body on a table in their lab.

This time I stumped him. He had nothing to say. In fact, he laughed because he knew I knew what I was talking about, and he knew he wasn't going to win with me.

He finally agreed to talk to Evan's psychiatrist. I had spoken with his psychiatrist prior to this, and he said he felt Evan's death was an accident. In all the times he had met with Evan, never once did he feel he was suicidal. In fact, *he too thought it was the choking game.* He agreed to contact the lead coroner.

Several minutes went by, and I received a call from the psychiatrist. He said he spoke with the lead coroner, who agreed to change the cause of death to "accidental." I was elated.

I felt so relieved and thanked him for helping me. He said that I had done all the work. The coroner just wanted to confirm it with him and said he already had planned to change it after speaking with me but just wanted to be able to document speaking with the psychiatrist. I broke into tears. They were tears of relief and tears of sadness. After I got off the phone I fell to my knees and thanked God for helping me. I knew I hadn't done this on my own. I felt led by God and by Evan. They helped me discover the truth.

To celebrate getting the cause changed to "accidental asphyxiation," I decided to tie blue ribbons around my mailbox and front yard trees. A neighborhood friend had a similar idea but to celebrate Evan's half birthday, which was July 15th.

Before I knew it, our neighborhood was covered in blue ribbons for Evan. It truly was a beautiful sight to see.

Some neighborhood friends got together and arranged to have a memorial placed for Evan at the end of our street. They planted a tree and did some landscaping. They also placed a bench and a memorial plaque. It was so beautiful. They also organized a celebration for Evan, and many people decorated their yards. One neighbor even spelled "Evan" in their front yard with lights. People wrote notes on balloons and lanterns and did a release at dusk. It was such a touching and beautiful event.

Some parents of Evan's friends got together and made a memorial at the local park. They too planted a tree with a plaque and bench and called it "Evan's Place where Everyone Is Valued, Accepted, and Needed ... EVAN." A student from the middle school made up this acronym, and it was so fitting.

As nice as it was to see these reminders of our sweet boy, it was still very hard. Even though friends and neighbors had done these things for us, I still felt very much alone in my sea of grief. I was drowning, and no one could save me.

I was also in constant contact with the local police department. Even though we found out Evan's death was an accident, we still had a lot of unanswered questions. The police had questioned a few people, but no one admitted to knowing what happened.

The bus driver said she overheard Evan and his friends talking about getting together as they got off the bus, but the boys were adamant that they didn't know anything about the choking game. I knew that someone had to know something, and they were just too afraid to speak up. Maybe they were afraid of getting in trouble, but I just wanted to know what happened and how Evan found out about the choking game.

I still had this feeling that the bully had something to do with it. I didn't have any actual proof, but I just knew he was involved. I asked the police to question him, but they didn't want to and said there was nothing they could do. They said he was just a kid. I knew he was just a kid but if he had something to do with it, I wanted to know. I contacted the chief of police and told him that if they didn't question the kid, I would do it myself and contact the local news. The chief agreed to have the bully questioned.

The lieutenant questioned the boy and his father, and the boy denied knowing anything. The boy lied about something, and the lieutenant knew but did not call him out. He asked the boy about the time he told Evan that he tried to hang himself. The boy denied that he had said this, and told the lieutenant that it was Evan who tried to hang himself. They knew it was a lie because the boy's mother had confirmed she put him in therapy after she was notified by the school.

96

I was very upset that the police didn't do more. I didn't understand why they let the bully get away with lying. If the bully would lie about that, then he would probably lie about the choking game too. The lieutenant actually said to me, "Why would he lie to the police?" I replied that people lie to the police all the time to avoid getting in trouble. How could he think the bully wouldn't lie to him, especially after he already lied once? The lieutenant asked me what I expected him to do, saying he couldn't arrest him. I knew that, but what I didn't understand is why he didn't tell him he knew he had lied. They were just going to let the boy get away with it. My son was dead, and nothing was being done about it.

Once we had the cause of death changed, I contacted the school and asked them to send a revised email to the district stating that Evan died from the choking game and not suicide. I felt it was not only important for the truth to be known but also to warn other parents so they could talk to their children about the dangers. If Evan knew about the choking game, then others had to know about it as well.

I was told that the school board did not feel it was beneficial to the district to send the email. They said that although we still paid taxes, we no longer had children in the district. We had decided to send Ava to Catholic school in the fall, and that seemed to offend some people. We no longer trusted the district, and we certainly weren't going to continue to send Ava there, especially when they refused to send a corrected email. I was actually told that they were going to leave it up to me to let people know what really happened to Evan. I couldn't believe the audacity of them to say that to me. I was angry and hurt.

My husband and I had been trying to work with the school to make policy changes and to bring programs into the school to help with mental health. We wanted to make sure that another child would never have to go through what Evan and our family went through. We reached out to our local state representative, and he was very willing to help us in any way he could.

We met with the local chapter of NAMI, the National Alliance on Mental Illness. They offer many free services and programs for mental health. They were very willing to go into the school and talk to students, teachers, and staff. The school agreed to have a speaker come in and speak to the staff but not the students. We really tried hard to make changes but were met with resistance from the school. The little bit that the school did do I felt was just to appease us, and they were still unwilling to speak about the choking game.

A couple of months after Evan passed away, we were contacted by a school administrator and asked to meet with her. She asked if we could meet at our home or at the elementary school. She did not want to meet at the middle school or the administration office. We thought it was odd, but we agreed to meet at the elementary school. We asked an education advocate and a couple of friends to join us, mainly for support but also to have witnesses. She wanted to know what happened with Evan during the school year. We told her everything, and she looked shocked. She proceeded to tell us that she would've given Evan a modified schedule and that she had just done it for another student recently.

I was so angry and shocked. I wanted to scream at her and tell her it was too little too late. She told us that she was going to investigate the issues with the bus driver. She later got back to us and told us that the principal never contacted the bus driver like she told us she would. She also had the bus driver fill out a form, and the driver commented that our son was annoying. We were told the bus driver was punished, but they couldn't tell us how. We were also informed that the bus driver was best friends with a school board member, so we figured nothing was ever done about the issue. The administrator never admitted any blame on the school's part, but I could tell she knew they were at fault. And once she realized it, her whole attitude toward us changed. She lied to our faces and covered things up.

That is one thing that district does well.

Many people had been telling us to consult a lawyer, but we really didn't want to do it. All we wanted was for changes to be made to school policies and for them to send a corrected email to the district. There was no amount of money that would ever make up for the loss of our son, but we felt the school needed to be held accountable.

We met with one law firm, but they wanted us to say that Evan died by suicide because it would look better for the case. I had just fought for the truth and wasn't about to do that, so we declined. We were told about another law firm that handled cases involving education and decided to meet with them. They seemed to be knowledgeable, so we wanted to see what they could do for us.

They requested all of Evan's records from the school and reviewed them. The lawyer told us that, based on what they reviewed, they felt we had a good case. She said there was so much evidence that the school did not provide Evan with the services he needed that, had we consulted them when he was alive, we would've won the case with no problem. However, now that he was deceased, we'd have to prove that his death was caused by the school's negligence.

We were told that it would be a long and painful process, and we just didn't want to go through that. The school's lawyer had told our lawyer that it was laughable we even consulted a lawyer. After that kind of a statement, I knew we would be dealing with heartless people, and we didn't need more pain. We knew they were wrong whether they admitted it or not, and money was not what we wanted. We wanted changes made to help other children like Evan. I really wish I would've known about an education lawyer before losing my son. Maybe things could've turned out differently.

Chapter 7

Months after Evan passed, I still struggled to make it through each day. I had my daughter to take care of, but I missed Evan so very much. I wanted to know where he was and if he was okay. I had faith that God had him and was taking care of him, but I needed to know. I started learning about near-death experiences because the people who had them saw a glimpse of what heaven was like.

I read books on near-death experiences; then I started reading books about mediums. I had always heard of this stuff and knew people who had seen mediums, but I'd never believed in any of it. I grew up Catholic and had always been told that that type of spirituality was "evil" and went against God, so it scared me. My sister-in-law, Katie, asked me if I would like to go with her to see a medium. I was nervous, but curious. My husband was even more skeptical, but he agreed to go with us.

We went to a spiritual town in New York called Lily Dale. It was a quaint little place with a peaceful vibe, full of old homes and shops. Katie had done some research and made appointments with a highly recommended medium. The day before we went Katie called me saying she had something big to tell me, but she wanted to wait until we got in town to tell us. I had no idea what it could be about, but she sounded very excited, so I was curious.

When we got there, Katie proceeded to tell us about an encounter she had had with someone she worked with. She had just moved back to Erie, Pa., before Evan passed away and had recently started working at a local hospital. Her office had to have some work done to it, so she was moved to a different part of the building. She didn't know anyone there at that point, and hadn't told anyone about what happened to Evan.

One day, a coworker asked her if she was feeling okay because her aura was gray and normally it was blue. She had no idea what the woman was talking about, so she just said she was fine. Later that day, the woman came up to her and handed her three Post-it notes. She said she was a medium but didn't like to tell people. She said she was getting messages from a boy, and she felt they were for his mother. She told Katie that while she was driving in her car the song "See You Again" by Whiz Khalifa came on the radio, and immediately, she started getting these messages. The interesting thing about that song is that it played a lot over the summer before we lost Evan when we were on vacation at the Outer Banks. After losing Evan, I started hearing it all the time. It became my song for Evan. There was no way this woman could've known that. She didn't know me at all and barely knew my sister-in-law.

The messages on the Post-it notes were unbelievable. I had no idea how this woman would've had any of that information. The first note said that mom is looking for signs, "I'm okay." It also said that he plays certain songs and "the person that looked like him was a glimpse of him."

102

I knew that Evan was letting me know he was okay, and I completely understood the part about the songs. I noticed early on that certain songs would come on at the perfect time. One time, I was in the car with Ava, and a certain song that she liked came on. When it was over, she said she wanted to hear it again. I tried explaining that I couldn't make it come on the radio again, but she insisted that I change the station, so I did. Sure enough, that song started playing again on the next channel. I remember thanking Evan for that and for saving me from one of Ava's temper tantrums. At the time, I wasn't really sure if it was him or just a coincidence—but now I knew for sure it was him.

We weren't exactly sure about the person who looked like him. I had seen someone who looked like Evan from afar but wasn't sure if that was what they were talking about. Or maybe it was that as Ava has gotten older, she looks a lot like Evan. I have always said what a blessing it is to see him too when I look at Ava.

The second note said, "betrayed, taken advantage of, wasn't intentional and friends drug use." This one really hurt. All I could think about is how Evan had told me the bully was being nice to him and then a couple of weeks later he died. I just knew it meant that Evan only did the dare because he thought the bully would accept him. And he confirmed that it was an accident. I knew it was an accident and that's why I fought to have his cause of death changed to accidental and now Evan was confirming it. By now I was in tears. I couldn't believe what I was reading.

The third note stated that she felt there were two different energies coming through. It said, "playing sports again, impulse, sorry, sorry, sorry, being selfish, prankster, moves stuff in house and December connection." Evan never played sports, so we figured that wasn't from him but the rest of it made sense to me. He was sorry that he did what he did. He was impulsive and decided to try it on his own instead of waiting for his friends. Evan was a prankster and I had noticed things moved around or missing and so did other family members. And lastly, the December connection. *Ava's and my birthdays are both in December.*

I couldn't believe it. Maybe all along it was Evan. He was just as persistent in spirit as he had been in his human form, and he wanted us to know he was okay and still with us.

The next day we went to Lily Dale. I was still in shock from the night before and couldn't imagine what else to expect. I was very nervous but excited. Immediately, Evan came through. The medium said that Evan was with my Gramma and that they are always with me. She described Evan exactly the way he was. She described his clothes, his mannerisms—even the snacks he liked. She said that he transitioned quickly and was helping my Gramma who had passed away nine years before Evan did. She even described my Gramma's personality.

She then told me that Evan was going to my father to put love in his heart. She said Evan never understood why he wasn't in my life. I was confused and didn't know how she could've known anything about my dad. I explained that my parents had been divorced since I was a baby, and I didn't know my dad. I knew that my dad was still alive and where he was living, but that was it. She said that Evan was working on him and that someday he would be in my life. I really didn't know what to think about any of that. I didn't know what to think about anything anymore. My life was so different now.

Over the summer, a classmate of Evan's reached out to me on Facebook. I had never heard of this boy before, but I replied to him. He told me that he didn't believe Evan killed himself on purpose. I told him that we already knew it was an accident and asked him what he meant by that. He proceeded to tell me that the day before Evan died, he overheard the bully talking to Evan at the lockers. He said the bully told Evan to tie one end of a rope to a tree and the other end around his neck. He claimed he had never heard of the choking game, but I later found out that it goes by many different names, so it's possible he knew it by another name.

He also told me some things that I never knew. Apparently, there was a lot more bullying going on than what Evan told me. He gave me the names of the students and told me that they would shove Evan in the halls and pull his chair out from under him. I thought Evan had been telling me everything, and now I felt awful that I never knew just how bad things were. He also told me that some of the middle school kids were doing drugs. I guess maybe that is what the medium meant by "drug use" in the note she gave my sister-in-law.

I always felt that this boy too was involved in some way and then reached out to me because he felt guilty. I imagine it took some courage for him to contact me, and I admired him for that. I kept in touch with this boy for a few years even after he transferred to a different school the following year. Things didn't appear to be going well for him, and eventually, I stopped hearing from him.

Earlier I mentioned that Evan had pointed out to me that he was wearing a watch. When we got it back after he passed, it was stopped in stopwatch mode. I always thought that he may have used it to try to time himself to stop himself before he passed out. My husband put the watch on top of the desk hutch so no one could reach it.

Several months later, he had a sudden urge to take the watch off the hutch. When he took it down, he noticed it was running nonstop in stopwatch mode. We thought it was odd because no one had touched it for months, and it wasn't running when he put it up there. We thought maybe somehow Evan had done something to it, but we never said anything to anyone about it because we figured people would think we were crazy. I put the watch in a drawer for safekeeping because I knew it was important.

One day my aunt asked me to look at model homes with her. I still wasn't going out a lot, but occasionally, I would try to get out of the house. The place she wanted to go to was closed, but we saw a sign for another one a little further down the road. I noticed someone pulling in behind us, but I didn't pay much attention. We looked around the house for a while and then went back to where the sales representative was. She was speaking to the woman who came in after us. We all started talking, and then the woman said to me that she was a medium and my son was standing right behind me. She told me that Evan liked to touch my hair and he was touching it right then. I had been noticing for some time that occasionally I would get a tingling sensation on my head. It was kind of like chills but in only one spot. I had never experienced anything like that before.

As she said that to me, I felt the tingling sensation on my head. She told me that this sensation was Evan touching me.

The medium also mentioned that he was with my Gramma, who was protecting him and telling her that she would never let anyone hurt him again. She said that when Evan passed away my Gramma was there with him. She walked him over to the other side and has been with him ever since. Evan also told her that his death was an accident, and he didn't know he was going to die. After his soul left his body, he stood over it, shaking his head in confusion. He didn't understand what had happened.

Then, she asked me if something recently happened to a clock or something that tells time. Evan was showing her that he had done something to a watch or clock. I couldn't believe what I heard. My legs felt weak and I almost fell over. I started crying. We never told anyone about the watch running in nonstop stopwatch mode. How could she have possibly known? I told her about the watch, and she said Evan did it.

As I write this, that watch is still running nonstop in stopwatch mode. It's been six years. I looked up the life span of a watch battery, and everything I read said that a regular watch battery only lasts about two years. A really good battery can last up to five years. The watch wasn't new when Evan got it from someone else, so it lasted well beyond the normal lifespan. I keep the watch in a safe place, and I look at it every now and then. It's a reminder to me that Evan is still very much alive and with us even though I can't see him.

I still keep in touch with Terri, the local medium, and we have gotten together several times. I even had her over to do a clearing in our current home. Evan has also sent other mediums to me over the years. I met one of them on a Facebook page, and we keep in touch as well. I have been told by several mediums that Evan is an exceptionally strong, persistent spirit. He always finds people who can deliver messages to me. He always makes sure to tell them that his death was an accident. I feel like that has been his most important message. It was so important to him that we knew he didn't leave us on purpose.

I feel that these people are gifts from God. They have helped me so much over the years. It's so hard to live without my sweet boy, but these special people have helped me to see that Evan is still here. It may not be in the way I want but at least he is here, and I can still have a relationship with him.

Earlier, I mentioned that a medium told me I would eventually meet my dad. I knew where he was living and found him on Facebook. One day I got this feeling that I should contact him, so I did. I was afraid of how he would react and thought maybe he wouldn't even respond. But he contacted me immediately and was happy to hear from me. It turns out that he had seen a medium, and they told him he would eventually see his kids. His wife had passed away and he was living alone in California. He decided to sell his house and move back east so he could be near us.

It was very nice getting to know my dad and spending time with him. He was heartbroken when I told him about Evan and said he wished he could've taken him fishing. I only got to spend a little over four years with him before he passed away, but I was happy I got to know him. Shortly after he passed away, he came through to one of my friends. She said she could see that he and Evan were together by a lake fishing and the sun was gold. I had never told anyone what my dad had said, and there was no way she could've known that. I knew that was my dad's way of letting me know he had finally met his grandson.

Chapter 8

There is nothing that I can do now to save my son, but I can save other children by spreading awareness and sharing Evan's story. He has told a couple of different mediums that I am meant to stay here on earth to help others and save lives. I promised him that I would do my very best to save others from this heartache.

Early on, while I was researching the choking game, I came across Erik's Cause, and I reached out to Judy Rogg, the director. She co-founded the non-profit organization after she lost her 12-year-old son, Erik, to the choking game in 2010. It has been her mission to spread awareness about the pass-out challenges and to save lives. She has also developed a non-graphic skill-based training program that can be used in schools for children ages nine to 18. It helps children build skills to help them say no to risk-taking behaviors. The program has been designed in a way that makes it easy for anyone to present. They also offer education for parents to help them talk to their children about the choking game and other difficult topics. For more information, go to www.erikscause.org.

In the six years that Evan has been gone, I have made it a mission of mine to spread awareness and educate others about the dangers of the deadly pass-out games. Mental health and bullying are also topics that are very important to me but are often overlooked.

As I mentioned earlier, Evan had been diagnosed with ADHD, anxiety, and high-functioning autism. I feel that all these diagnoses played a significant role in his tragic death. In addition, the school did not do enough to help him with his anxiety that was triggered in the classroom. His anxiety was also exacerbated by the lack of action in response to bullying—in my view, they did not take the bullying seriously enough. Instead, they kept insisting that Evan was "fine" because he was well-behaved and had good grades.

In reality, my son was not fine—instead of acting out, he suffered in silence. He had stopped calling out his bullies, because it seemed like it made no difference. I believe that schools should know that academics are not always an indicator of mental health and good grades do not mean that everything is fine. Schools need to trust and listen to what the parents are saying. In my opinion, the mental health and well-being of a child are far more important than academics.

According to the Centers for Disease Control and Prevention, ADHD, anxiety, and behavior disorders are the more common disorders that are diagnosed in children. Per the CDC, from 2016–2019, children from the ages of three to 17 years of age have been diagnosed with the following:[1]

- 9.8% ADHD
- 9.4% anxiety
- 8.9% behavior problems
- 4.4% depression

It is also very common for children to have more than one of the above diagnoses. If these diagnoses are made early and the children and their families receive the proper services, it can make a difference in their lives. If a child receives the proper mental health care, it can help them to learn better, handle their emotions and stress, and give them the confidence they need to make healthy choices.

Bullying is another problem for today's youth. Per the CDC, bullying is defined as having the three following elements:[2]

- Unwanted aggressive behavior

---

[1] "What are common childhood mental disorders?" *Children's Mental Health*. Last reviewed June 28,2021.
https://www.cdc.gov/mentalhealth/tools-resources/children/index.htm

[2] "What is bullying?" *Preventing Bullying*. Last reviewed October 3, 2019. https://www.cdc.gov/violenceprevention/pdf/bullying-factsheet508.pdf

- Observed or perceived imbalance of power
- Repetition or high likelihood of repetition of bullying behaviors

The different types of bullying are physical, verbal, social, and cyber. According to stopbullying.gov, 90% of children in grades four to eight reported that they have been harassed or bullied and 20% in grades 9–12. It is also noted that 64% of students who are bullied do not report it.[3]

Bullying affects everyone involved, and it can lead to increased anxiety and missed school days. Children with disabilities are often more at risk of being bullied. I have talked to many kids from my son's school, and they have told me that the bullying has continued, and they feel that the school really doesn't care about them. Several of his classmates told me that they saw Evan getting shoved in the halls, having his chair pulled out from under him, etc. They said they never told anyone because they knew nothing would be done about it. Years later, these kids feel guilty for not speaking up and telling anyone. I know they were just kids themselves, and it's not their fault. It's a shame that the kids don't think anyone cares about what happens to them, and I blame the adults.

------

[3] "What is bullying?" *Frequency of Bullying.* Last reviewed June 30,2022. https://www.stopbullying.gov/bullying/what-is-bullying#frequency

Schools will say they have a zero-tolerance policy when it comes to bullying, but from what I have seen, it's just words on a piece of paper.

As I mentioned earlier, my husband and I had never heard of the choking game before losing our son. We found out that it has been around for approximately 100 years, and the way it is "played" has changed over time, making it even more deadly and dangerous. Social media has allowed it to reach far more children than it ever had in the past.

According to Erik's Cause (a nonprofit charitable organization dedicated to spreading awareness about the dangers of the pass-out games), the choking game or pass-out challenges are activities that involve cutting off the oxygen supply to the brain by compression of carotid arteries, chest compressions after hyperventilation, or the tap-out/submission hold. This causes a tingling, euphoric feeling that can last several seconds prior to losing consciousness. Because these activities are presented as a game, many kids do not realize they can be seriously injured or even lose their lives. These activities used to be "played" in groups, but now are being tried alone using a rope, belt, or scarf. Because there is no way to know when they will lose consciousness, they pass out and accidentally choke to death.

Currently, there are no accurate statistics for deaths and injuries related to the pass-out challenges. This is because there are no death or injury codes for these activities. And many deaths are misclassified as suicide because there is no set way for coroners and police to determine the choking game as the cause.

The children who participate in these activities are usually between the ages of 9–16. Many children do it because they are curious or are pressured to try it by their peers. We believe Evan tried it because of peer pressure. He wanted to fit in, and he thought that the bully would finally accept him if he tried the dare. Just like many other children, Evan thought it was safe because the other kids were doing it, and nothing happened to them. I wish I had known about the choking game sooner, so I would've had the opportunity to talk to Evan and tell him how dangerous it is.

Over the years, my husband and I have done many things to help spread awareness about the choking game, mental health, and bullying.

As I mentioned earlier, we tried to get the school to make changes, which proved to be difficult. In May 2016, I spoke at a school board meeting about mental health. It was very hard to do, seeing as how it had only been two months after we had lost Evan, but I felt it was important for me to do. After the meeting, someone from the board came up to me and told me that I was a glutton for punishment and that they knew all about anxiety. They proceeded to tell me that when their sibling acted crazy, they would tell them to go and take a pill. I couldn't even respond to them because I was in complete shock that they would even say something like that to me. Another board member came up to me and said that they heard me to which I said, "I don't need you to just hear me. I need you to actually do something about it." He just looked at me and then put his head down.

116

At the beginning of the meeting, the board announced that they were going to have a student do a reading that she had done for the Speech and Debate national competition. Prior to the reading, it was announced that it was very emotional and may be upsetting to some. The poem was written by Meggie Royer and titled The Morning After I Killed Myself. By this time, we already knew that Evan's death was an accident but hearing the poem was very upsetting to me. I was experiencing depression and anxiety and really felt that poem. I could feel tears welling up in my eyes, and I started shaking and sobbing. I couldn't take it anymore, and I jumped up and ran outside.

A few people came running after me. The next thing I knew, the student who was doing the reading came outside with her mother, and they were both crying and really upset. The school never told her that I would be there that night, and she felt so bad that it upset me. While we were outside, several parents told the board how horrible they were for upsetting me and the student. All they would say about it was that they warned us it could be upsetting to some. The district just kept proving to us over and over how heartless they really were.

I still got up and did my speech about mental health. I was not about to let their ignorance hold me back.

I mentioned earlier that my husband and I had reached out to our local state representative. He was willing to work with us and wanted to put a spotlight on mental health. He organized a Mental Health Symposium, and we set up an information table about the choking

117

game. We invited the local news station, and they interviewed my husband and me, as well as the local state representative. We had a solid turnout and felt like our message reached a lot of people. Even though it was painful for us to see certain staff members from the school, we were still glad that they attended. The whole experience was empowering for both my husband and me, and we hoped to do the symposium again the following year. Unfortunately, the representative that was elected the following year never followed through with it. We were disappointed, but still determined.

Over the summer, we had a gathering near one of Evan's memorials in a local park—I was glad to see Evan's classmates, a few of his teachers, friends, and family there. We had snacks, and the Kona Ice truck came. I had made some signs and put together some activities for the kids about bullying and kindness, and I think people appreciated what we were doing. We just wanted to encourage the kids to be kind to one another and to stick up for each other. We wanted them to be inspired by Evan's kindness to others and follow in his footsteps. We had a very nice turnout but were still inspired to reach more people.

In April of 2017, my husband and I, and Judy Rogg from Erik's Cause, put together a free seminar called "The Dangers of Deadly Pass-Out Challenges." We invited local area school districts, law enforcement, doctors and their staff, and more people from the community. We had around 15 people show up, which was a decent turnout, but I wanted to see more. At least we were trying to do something. It gave me purpose. It gave me another reason to keep going.

At times I wanted to give up. It was hard to keep pushing myself. Sometimes, I had to take a break from all of it. I needed to have time to rest and time to just cry and grieve for my son. Each time I would come back stronger. I would always think about Evan and knew he was cheering us on. He wanted us to do this, and we wanted to do it for him.

The following year, my husband was invited to speak at the American Mental Wellness Association Conference. His speech was called "The Boy with The Helicopter in His Head and The School Who Failed Him." When he shared Evan's story, there was not a dry eye in the room. A few months later, we were contacted by someone who had heard this talk. She was moved by our story and invited us to speak at a school and student safety conference for 13 school districts. We were happy to be invited to share our story again.

Over the years, I have done a few interviews with local news stations about the choking game and bullying. Every chance I get, I share Evan's story. I wrote an article for *Love What Matters*, and Evan's name and picture are included in a 2018 *Time Magazine* article about the choking game. I have spoken at my daughter's school on two separate occasions, and I hope to do it again.

Evan had made up his own drink at Starbucks, which we called "the Evan Special." One day, my daughter and I were at a local Starbucks, and we told the barista about Evan and how he made up his own drink. We asked if it was possible to have his drink named after him. She said she would talk to her manager. Much to our surprise, she contacted me to let me know they were going to do it. The manager invited us to meet with her and see the sign they made. They named it "Evan's Special." They have had it on their menu for over a year now, and it's a popular drink.

The manager has allowed me to set up an informational table about the choking game in that Starbucks several times. I've spoken with many people while there and have had several kids tell me that they have heard of the choking game, know someone who has done it or have seen it as a challenge on TikTok and other social media platforms. I tried reaching out to a couple of local schools, but unfortunately never received a reply.

I'll never understand why so many schools are afraid and unwilling to warn students and parents about the dangers.

I am always so surprised by the number of adults who tell me that they used to do it with their friends when they were younger. They say that at the time, they had no idea how dangerous it was or that they could've died from it. I've also had people tell me that their children would never do such a thing because they are good kids and smart. I always say that the biggest mistake you can make is to think *not my kid, they'd never do that.*

Even smart kids can make bad choices.

120

It is important to remember that children's brains are not fully developed until age 25. They can have a false sense of safety and believe they are invincible. As parents, we need to have open dialogues with our children and push ourselves to have uncomfortable conversations. Knowledge is power and educating children at home is so important for keeping them safe.

Chapter 9

Grief is a concept that I never used to give much thought to. I knew it was a word used in relation to the loss of a loved one, but it was something unfamiliar to me. I was lucky enough to make it to adulthood before understanding this word, and I really didn't understand it until I lost my sweet boy.

Grief is defined as the deep sorrow one feels as a result of the loss of a loved one. Some have said that grief is a measure of the amount of love you have for the person you have lost. The more love you have for someone, the more grief you will feel. Grief can look different to different people, and there truly is no handbook for it. Everyone experiences grief in their own way.

My grandfather passed away when I was 23 years old, and he was the first person I ever lost who was close to me. He was a father figure to me, and when he passed away at the age of 68, I was devastated. I had never felt such sadness, and death was very unfamiliar to me. All I knew was that I was never going to see him again. I watched my grandmother grieve for him. She stopped wanting to go places and do things that she did while he was alive. I remember thinking that he would want her to keep living and enjoying life, but I never truly understood just how difficult that was at the time.

My grandmother passed away 11 years after my grandfather, and I struggled. I was very close to my grandmother, and I couldn't imagine not being able to talk to her again. Evan was only three at the time, and he was close to her too. We explained that GG went to heaven, and she was way up in the sky. He thought he could fly in a rocket ship to visit her. I wish that was possible, especially now. There was a chair in our house that my Gramma always sat in. After she died, Evan would get upset if someone sat in her chair. He'd tell us that GG was sitting there. I just thought he didn't want anyone to sit in the chair she used to sit in. Knowing what I know now, I believe Evan really did see my Gramma sitting there.

The grief that I feel for Evan is completely different than the grief I felt for my grandparents. You *expect* to lose your grandparents and parents at some point. That is the way things are meant to be. You never expect to lose a child, especially at such a young age. As parents, we are supposed to take care of our children and protect them. We aren't supposed to have to plan a funeral for them. We shouldn't ever have to see their lifeless little body in a coffin and then never see them or hold them again. That is not the normal progression of life, yet it happens.

It happened to me and my husband—and it has happened to many other parents.

I can't describe the pain of child loss. There are no words in the English dictionary that can even come close to the pain I feel every day of my life. I miss my sweet boy so much, and I long to see his sweet face and kiss the little freckles on his nose. I miss feeling his warmth and holding his hand. I miss his hugs and hearing him say, "I love you, Mommy." He was in my life every single day, I was taking care of him, and then one day he was just gone. Some days are harder to get through than others, and I really don't know why. The pain will just knock the wind right out of me, and I never even see it coming. I did so much for Evan, and after I lost him, I just didn't know what to do with myself.

Yes, I still had Ava to take care of, but she never needed me the way Evan did. Ava did not have the struggles that Evan had. She was very independent and wanted to do things by herself. He depended heavily on me, and after I lost him, I felt I no longer had a purpose in this world.

Grief makes us feel alone and misunderstood. After Evan died, I found myself living in a world I no longer recognized—I didn't even recognize myself. I tried to do the things I always did and to be around people I knew, but I just never felt like I fit in or belonged. I was different and I didn't even know how to be around myself. I didn't even *want* to be around myself.

If there was a way for me to escape, I would've done it.

I felt like I had nothing in common with my friends anymore. They had no idea the extreme amount of pain I was in, and they couldn't understand it.

I found it was easier to just stay home alone. I could cry and not feel bad about making someone uncomfortable.

People didn't want to hear me talk about my dead child, and they didn't want to see me cry. I could tell by their facial expressions that I was making them uncomfortable. They didn't understand that I was uncomfortable all the time. I was uncomfortable around myself. All I wanted was to have my son back and feel normal again. I wanted to fit in again.

I was raised in a Catholic family, and I went to Catholic school from kindergarten through college. I knew there was a heaven, and I knew there was an afterlife, but I didn't really understand what that meant. Now that my son was there, I needed to find out more.

I believed in signs, but I was also skeptical. Could spirits really communicate with us, or was it just our imagination? Or was it the devil playing tricks on us? I can't say that I fully understand how spirits are able to communicate with us, but what I do know is that the signs bring me happiness and hope.

I had a few experiences in my life that made me think it was possible, and my Gramma had shared some of her experiences with me over the years. After she passed away, I was taking a nap on the couch, and I woke up to the feeling of someone stroking my hand. I can still feel it to this day. I had thought maybe it was my Gramma comforting me. I also had a couple of visitation dreams from her. They were always comforting, and she looked happy. I didn't know how it was possible, but I believed it was her.

I had another visitation dream from my Gramma shortly after Evan's funeral. I was walking alone in a field of grass, and suddenly, I saw her sitting in the chair she always sat in at my house. She had a couple of men who looked Italian standing behind her chair. I didn't recognize them but felt they were family. She looked so pretty and had this peaceful look on her face. I went to her and kneeled and put my head in her lap. I could feel her, and I felt such peace and happiness. I asked what she was doing there, and she said, "Evan is with a neighbor and God is watching him." I asked why she wasn't with him but then I woke up. I felt it was her letting me know that Evan was okay and being taken care of. It brought me peace, but I still wanted Evan.

I have had several visitation dreams from Evan over the years. They are just so amazing. In those dreams, I feel the happiness I once had when he was alive. I can feel his warmth when I hug him and feel his long lashes brush against my cheek. I am always aware that he is only visiting and can't stay. I never see his lips move when he is talking, yet I can hear what he is saying. It's like I can hear him in my mind. I wake up crying because I am so happy. Sometimes I can hear him in my mind when I'm awake, and I see quick images in my mind. It's really hard for me to explain it, but I know it's him. A mother always knows her child, even in spirit.

A few days after Evan passed away, our priest came over to our house to go over funeral arrangements. We had a house full of people, so they all witnessed this. Matt and I walked Fr. Ben to the front door. Suddenly, the power went out. It sounded like everything electrical was powered down. I can't exactly describe how it sounded but I had never heard anything like it. We all just looked at each other. Then my friend Sabrina said, "Evan, knock it off," and the power came back on.

A few years later, Terri, the medium, and I were at her house sitting at her kitchen table and talking about Evan when the same thing happened. It sounded like all the power was just sucked out of the house. It happened a couple of times, and then suddenly the house it got cold. I had heard that it can get very cold when spirits are around, but I had never experienced it before. By this time, I was used to experiencing things like this, but early on, I was unsure. It didn't faze Terri at all—as a medium, she was used to these kinds of things.

In those early days, I started reading books about near-death experiences and mediums. Those books really helped me get a better understanding of where my son was and what things were like for him in heaven. I also learned to recognize signs from Evan, although I still doubted myself at times. His first signs had to do with electricity. I would notice lights flickering at home. We never had anything like that happen before we lost him. I started noticing lights flickering when we were on vacation or at other people's houses. And it always seemed to happen when we were talking about Evan, or I was thinking about him.

I started finding a ton of bird feathers everywhere I went. Evan used to pick up bird feathers and keep them. I would tell him not to touch them because they were full of germs, but he didn't listen. He always had a stash of feathers in my car and all over the house. I still have a bunch of his feathers that he had collected. I just knew the feathers we found were from Evan.

Over the years we have found all kinds of feathers in some unexpected places. Once I was sitting on the couch in the family room and a little white feather just floated down from above and landed right on me. Another medium friend asked Evan to send cardinal feathers to us because we had never found one of those. He told her he wanted to send us a blue jay feather because blue is the color of heaven and then he showed himself plucking a tail feather from a blue jay. Not long after that, we found a blue jay tail feather sticking straight up out of the ground at my father-in-law's house. That summer Ava ended up finding a bunch of cardinal feathers too. She had gotten upset about losing the first cardinal feather she found, so Evan sent her a few more. She was so excited. We now have stashes of feathers throughout the house and in my car. Evan definitely has a good sense of humor!

We've had so many amazing signs from Evan over the years that I could probably write a whole book about just about the signs! Here are a few more stories that really stand out to me.

On our first Christmas without Evan, we decided to go to Puerto Rico. Not only was it beautiful, but it also served as a much-needed distraction. Everywhere we went, we heard Spanish music or Christmas music. On Christmas Eve, we were walking through a little fishing village where people were out celebrating and playing Christmas music. Suddenly, my husband stopped walking and told us to listen. In the distance, we heard "Piano Man" playing. We realized it was coming from a golf cart that was parked on the street. Earlier, I mentioned that "Piano Man" was one of Evan's favorite songs and he loved golf carts. One wouldn't expect to hear that song in Puerto Rico, especially coming from a golf cart. We knew that was Evan letting us know he was with us.

A couple years later, we went back to Puerto Rico for Christmas with family. We decided to take a ferry ride over to Culebra. It was still dark out as we were lining up to get on the boat. As we got up to the boat, we were surprised to see that the name of the boat was "Mr. Evan." We came to find out that, at the last minute, they changed the boat. We were supposed to take the ferry but ended up on Mr. Evan. "Evan" is not a name you would expect to find in Puerto Rico, so once again we knew it was our sweet boy letting us know he was with us.

I've been lucky to have caught glimpses of Evan. Sometimes I can see a white movement out of the corner of my eye. The first time, I thought I was imagining it, but I soon realized it was Evan. It was when we were still living in our last house. I was inside alone. Matt was out back cutting the grass, and Ava went outside to play. I heard the alarm chime when she opened the door and walked out.

Out of the corner of my eye, I saw someone who I assumed was Ava running behind me. I was confused because I had just seen her walk by and go out the front door. If she came back in, I would've heard the alarm chime and would've seen her walk by. I turned around and called her name, but she didn't answer. I walked around looking for her in her usual hiding spots but couldn't find her. I honestly thought she was just playing with me, so I said, "okay Ava," and went back to what I was doing. Then, I happened to glance out the sunroom window and saw Ava swinging on the swing in the backyard. There was no way that was her in the house. I ran out back and asked Ava if she had just been inside the house, and she said no. I was frantic and I guess I scared her because she started crying. I told Matt what had happened. I think he believed me, but I think he also was skeptical.

I caught glimpses of Evan a few more times at our new house—and my husband even saw him once. He finally believed me because he'd seen Evan with his own eyes. Matt hasn't had as many experiences, but he has had a few and has had a visitation dream or two. Ava has had dreams and has seen orbs. One time, Ava and I were lying in bed, and we both saw a bright white light zoom across the ceiling. I had never seen anything like it in my life, but I knew it was Evan. I could just feel him, and I started crying. Ava had seen an orb floating around the bed at our last house, but I didn't see it that time. She woke me up crying because it scared her. I told her that she didn't need to be scared because it was just Evan checking up on her.

I have been very blessed to receive so many signs and messages from Evan. He tries so hard to let me know he's still here, but I still struggle. It's just not the same, but if it must be this way, then I'm thankful to be able to still have a relationship with him.

I still have days where the grief is so heavy that it makes it hard to function. On those days I try to remember

131

all the signs that Evan has sent me. It helps me a lot to talk about the signs because it reminds me that Evan is still very much alive and with me. And I do know he is still here, but some days, that is just not enough.

I will sit quietly and talk to him in my mind, and sometimes I will hear him, but often I can feel him touch my hair. I feel him just about every day, and that does bring me some comfort, but it will never be the same as having him here with me in person. Nothing compares to being able to see his sweet face and hug him and feel his warmth. There are some days I just have to sit and cry and let it out. I try to remind myself that there will be better days, not every day will hurt as bad. And when I am having a good day, I try to enjoy it and hold on to it because those days are special.

I am always going to grieve my son and miss him until the day we are reunited. I have okay days and bad days and a lot of in-between days. I imagine it'll always be like that. I have moments of happiness, but there is always that sadness from missing Evan. I'm always wondering what he would be doing now and how he would be with Ava. I miss having both of my babies here with me. Ava misses her brother, too, although she said she hardly remembers him now. She has a few memories, and we talk about him all the time and share stories. We do the best we can to keep him in the present and include him in our daily lives. He may live in heaven in his spirit form, but he will always be our son. And we will always be grateful that he chose us to be his family.

Chapter 10

Even though Evan is gone, he continues to make an impact on others. Many of his classmates have reached out to me over the years, and from the things they tell me, I can see how much he meant and still means to them. It is so very important to me that Evan is remembered and loved. I did not want his death to be in vain. I wanted his life to have meaning and purpose and for others to learn and make changes for the better. I never want to see another child have to go through what he did.

He has left behind a legacy of love and kindness, and because of him, others have learned to become kinder and more empathetic. It makes me so proud as his mother to see that he has had that kind of an effect on others. He was just a child, but he had the wisdom and the compassion of a very wise and old soul. And because of Evan, there will be kinder and more compassionate people in this world. That is a huge accomplishment for anyone, let alone a little boy. To say I am beyond proud of him is an understatement. He is one special child, and I'm thankful and blessed to call him my son.

A couple of months after losing Evan, a few of his friends' parents had a mass for him and a luncheon. It was so nice to see his friends and classmates. I really missed them. They gave us a beautiful book full of pictures and letters written by friends, classmates, and teachers. There were so many letters that not all of them fit in the book, so

133

they gave them to us in an envelope. The book cover was a picture of Evan walking on the playground, and the last page had the words to Billy Joel's "Piano Man." It was such a beautiful and special gift. I could hardly see the pages because I was crying, but I got to hug each and every one of the kids there. It felt so good to be able to wrap my arms around those 12-year-old kids, since I could no longer hug my own 12-year-old son.

It took me a while to be able to look at the book again. I cry every single time I look at the pictures and read the letters. I did this again recently and still cried, but this time, I also laughed and smiled. I learned so much about these kids and how they felt about Evan. I honestly don't think he ever knew just how much he meant to so many of them.

These letters were written when everyone thought Evan had died by suicide. These little kids were saying how bad they felt because they didn't know he was struggling, and if they knew, they would have helped him. Some kids wrote about how they had similar struggles and how they would talk to Evan about it. And others talked about his love of history and old things or how they had bonded over the game *Minecraft* or the Marvel comic character Deadpool. Another kid said he could've sworn that Evan was watching over him at the National History Bee. Others wrote about special memories with Evan—like the time he made the jukebox in the cafeteria play a song without using a quarter, or how Evan could spin in a circle really fast on his tire swing without getting dizzy or sick.

I would like to share a few quotes about Evan from his friends and classmates:

He made everything fun.

He was a good friend.

I also liked Evan's kindness.

He was always friendly and kind to me.

I promise I will treat people with respect and kindness.

I am forever a better person now, thanks to Evan.

I was truly amazed by what those kids wrote. They were just 12 years old, but their words were so meaningful; I was deeply touched that they knew so much about Evan. He had clearly made a connection with his classmates and touched their lives in such a beautiful way. It makes me happy knowing that they will always remember Evan's kindness. I imagine that most parents who have lost a child fear that the child will be forgotten, but I can see that Evan will always be remembered by his classmates. We will always treasure that beautiful book.

I've heard regularly from his classmates over the years. Many of them, I never knew prior to losing him, but some of them, I remembered from school. A couple of kids took up a collection in his name for a local cat rescue or made donations to a local animal shelter. They knew how much he loved animals, especially cats.

One classmate reached out to me saying she had issues at school too and that she thought about leaving this world. She said reading my posts on Facebook and seeing the pain I was in made her change her mind. She told me that she just couldn't put her mother through that.

I still keep in touch with her, and she is doing well.

Several kids told me that they were bullied and mistreated in school as well. Some of them told me things that happened to Evan, things I never knew. They felt bad for not sticking up for him or telling a teacher, but they honestly felt the school didn't care and wouldn't do anything about it. I think that is so sad. A school environment should be a place where the students feel safe and supported to learn and grow, but that is not how they felt. I've told them not to be hard on themselves. They were just kids.

I've heard from so many who said Evan was always smiling at people and holding the door open for others. They said that he always included everyone and would say encouraging words if someone was having a bad day. His classmates have told me that they make an effort to help others because of how Evan showed them kindness. They'll smile at people and hold the door open for others, and some have even stuck up for others. Evan has left such a beautiful legacy behind.

One of Evan's sixth-grade teachers would invite the students to have lunch with him in his classroom. He did this as a way for the kids to escape the cafeteria, especially if they were having a bad day. Evan never told us about this. We heard about it from some of the kids. He ate in the cafeteria most days but sometimes he would go up to the classroom. I was told later by two of his friends that he would sometimes invite them to go with him, especially if they were having a bad day. The one girl, Nakayla, I knew but the other girl, Courtney I did not know. They said they would play card games together, and Evan always beat them. They were grateful for Evan's friendship and kindness. The way they speak about him to this day warms my heart. He meant and still does mean so much to them.

I have kept in touch with a few of the kids but especially Nakayla and Courtney. I call them "Team Evan" because they have done so much in memory of him. They both have gotten tattoos for him and wear Evan bracelets I had made. They even included Evan in their senior photos.

A couple of the kids told me that when they are having a bad day, they will think about Evan and ask for his help. It is truly amazing to me how much these kids care about him. Of course, I know how wonderful and special Evan was and still is, but hearing the stories from these kids leaves me speechless. I always say Evan was a much better person than I am. He had a way of connecting with so many people. Even though he was struggling, he still made an effort to help others.

It helps me to know how much Evan means to others. I'm so very proud of him. When people think of Evan, they'll remember his smile and his kindness. Evan always talked about the Golden Rule: Do unto others as you would have them do unto you. It's really just that simple. If you wouldn't like something said or done to you, then you shouldn't say or do it to someone else. Evan never understood how some people could be so mean, and he didn't understand injustice and bullying. He was just nice to everyone—even to those who were not treating him kindly.

As parents, we want our children to be kind- and good-hearted people. We teach them manners and teach them to be empathetic and respectful. We teach them to stick up for others and for themselves. But I am not sure if everyone teaches their children these things. My son was not treated with the same kindness and compassion that he showed others, and that makes me sad.

I have struggled with my feelings over the years regarding the child who dared my son to play that game. I am conflicted because I know he was just a kid himself, and I know he too was suffering. I know he bullied Evan because he himself was struggling and that he thought it would help him to do to someone else what was being done to him. Several classmates said that this boy laughed and claimed not to care that Evan had passed away. This upset Evan's friends, and it obviously upset us. How could a child be so cruel and uncaring? It made me wonder what awful things were happening to him, and I can't help but feel there have been many missed opportunities for him as well. I imagine that it would be very difficult for a person, especially a child, to live with the fact that they share blame for the death of another child.

Evan's senior year of high school would have been 2022, the year this book was published. Early in that school year, I was contacted by the mother of one of Evan's friends. Her son was in a public speaking class with the bully. They were assigned to do a lighthearted speech about a pet or something they did over the summer. When he did his speech, he started by saying that he was the reason someone was no longer alive. He said he bullied and tormented someone, and now he has to live with the fact that that person died. He went on to say that he was against bullying, and hoped that if Evan were still alive, they could've been friends.

He then put up a picture of Evan. I was told that the class went silent. Not even the teacher spoke a word.

I had so many mixed emotions about this. I was glad that he had come to terms with what he had done, and that he took the blame for what happened to Evan, but it felt a little too late. Now he says they could've been friends, but when Evan tried to be his friend, the boy had treated him horribly. Over the years I had thought about how he laughed when he heard Evan had died. I was angry at him. Now he was showing some remorse, and I was, again, conflicted.

Then I became concerned about that boy's safety. I was worried that he might do something to hurt himself. Here I was now worrying about the boy who hurt my son! He was still a child, and I didn't want anything to happen to him. Another tragedy wouldn't make things better. I reached out to a teacher friend to make sure he was OK. I didn't hear anything else about him for the rest of that year.

Before I knew it, the end of the 2022 school year was upon us. It was very hard for me knowing that we would not be able to celebrate graduation with our son. We would've been so proud of him, and we would've had a huge graduation party for him. Now all I could do was make sure Evan was remembered at graduation. It was important to me that he was included, and it was important to his friends and classmates. I wanted Evan to be acknowledged, and he deserved to be included, especially after everything he went through. The least the school could do was honor him and acknowledge him as a part of the graduating class.

My friend Sabrina worked hard to make sure Evan would be included in the yearbook. She wouldn't take "no" for an answer. I was notified that there would be a memorial section for Evan in the senior section of the yearbook. I was ecstatic and couldn't believe the school was doing this for him, since they previously had never allowed anything to be done in his memory. Over the years the students weren't allowed to do anything for him. I always thought that if the school allowed the students to do something for Evan, maybe they thought that meant they were acknowledging their wrongdoing. Why else would they allow things to be done for the other students who had passed away after him? Evan deserved to be remembered just as much as the other students. I just knew Evan had something to do with his being included in the memorial section. Now I had to make sure he was remembered at graduation.

I had been talking to some of Evan's classmates and their parents, and they assured me that something would be done for him. One of my medium friends told me that Evan said he would be at graduation, and they were going to do something for him. I wanted to believe it, but I was so afraid the school wouldn't allow it.

A couple of weeks before graduation, I was contacted by a school administrator who wanted to invite my family to a special senior ceremony, as well as check that it was okay to include Evan's picture in the senior video they would be showing at graduation. I couldn't believe it. I hadn't talked to this person in years, but I was more than willing to do it if it meant my son would be included. She told me that every year the seniors decorate a column at the school. This year, there was a blue tulip on the column, and they were dedicating the color of the flower to Evan. The seniors would be signing the column, and we were invited to come to the school and sign it for Evan.

I was so happy and emotional. It meant the world to me, but I was anxious about having to interact with the administrator and prayed that God would give me strength.

As luck would have it, this administrator wasn't able to attend. I felt that someone up above had a hand in that, and I was relieved. Matt, Ava, and I proudly wore our Evan T-shirts. When I saw the beautiful column, I was overcome with emotion and started crying. I honestly didn't expect to be so emotional. I was proud, happy, and sad all at the same time. The blue tulip was beautiful and even had Evan's name hidden on the side. I proudly wrote "In Loving Memory of Evan William Ziemniak."

We were also invited to attend the actual graduation ceremony, but we declined. I just couldn't see how we could sit through it and then watch Evan's bully walk across the stage knowing he could be the reason our son wasn't there. I was torn though: Part of me wanted to go but part of me was afraid to go. I was afraid of how I would feel and act when seeing certain people. I just thought it would be too hard on my already broken heart.

Evan's friend Courtney contacted me before graduation—she was upset. She was one of the students pushing to have Evan included in the graduation ceremony. A friend of hers was one of the artists who worked on designing and painting the senior column. They had wanted to dedicate a blue tulip to Evan by putting his name on it but weren't allowed to do so. (They did it anyways, though ... which makes me smile.) His name may have been on the side of the flower, instead of front and center, but it was there. Courtney also asked to have a chair dedicated to Evan and present us with his diploma, but the school administrator wouldn't allow it.

I am so appreciative of all that Courtney and the class of 2022 did for Evan.

As graduation day got closer, I started having second thoughts about not going. What if I regretted not going? I reached out to a group of parents who had lost children and asked what I should do. So many of them shared with me their experiences of attending what should've been their child's graduation. They all said they were happy that they went. A friend of mine had invited Matt and me to go and sit with them. So, I really started considering it. I decided to decorate Evan's memorials for graduation, and I bought a class of 2022 picture frame and put Evan's picture in it.

I decided that I needed to go to graduation, and I was going to take Evan's picture with me. I am so glad we went. It was such an amazing experience. Yes, it was hard to see the bully graduate, but I felt so proud to be there for Evan. When they showed his pictures at the end of the video, people cheered and clapped for him. I proudly sat in the bleachers with Evan's picture sitting right next to me. After graduation, I waited because I wanted to see some of Evan's friends. Most of them had no idea that Matt and I would be there.

Courtney and her family were there. She was wearing her Evan bracelet and her family wore their Evan T-shirts. Another classmate and her mom decorated their car with blue ribbons, *In Loving Memory of Evan Ziemniak* was written on the back windshield. Evan's friend Anthony wore his Evan T-shirt under his gown. Another friend was surprised to see us but so happy and proud to show us that he had Evan's name on his cap, and his family decorated their car with blue ribbons. I got to hug so many of them and have my picture taken with them while holding Evan's photo. Many of them, I had not seen since they were still in middle school. They were all so grown up now, and many of them were taller than me. I think it was just as healing for them to see us as it was for us to see them. We felt the love for Evan and saw that he was important to them and remembered. It was an experience that I will never forget.

I asked a few of Evan's classmates and friends what he represents or means to them. Nakayla said that Evan was her friend who always had everyone's back even if they didn't have his. He taught her to be kinder, selfless, and genuine. "The world needs more people like him in it. People who are kind, do not judge others, and want nothing in return."

Courtney compared Evan to a rare coin, saying, "They are hard to find but you are lucky if you do." She also said "Evan was one of the kindest kids I knew. He never judged you or made you feel any less than others. I've done everything in my power to honor him because I know that is what he would've done for others."

Anthony said, "Evan inspired me to pursue foreign policy because of our shared fascination with history. He shaped my future quite literally. Evan was great to me and great to so many. He will always be in my memory and in my heart."

I have come to realize that Evan was never meant to stay in this life for a long time. He was here to teach a lesson, and that lesson is to be kind to others. I know that, because of him, people have changed for the better. I am in awe at how this sweet little boy with so many earthly struggles has made such an impactful impression on people. He continues to work through me. I promised him that I would continue to spread awareness about the choking game and mental health and that I would try my best to help others in his honor.

144

I must admit that this was a difficult chapter for me to write. I wanted to show what a good person Evan was and what a difference he has made in the lives of others, but I'm angry. I'm angry that my son had to die to change others for the better. Sometimes I'm angry at the kids. Why didn't anyone stand up for Evan the way he stood up for them? Why weren't they there for him the way he was there for them? I know they were just kids, but so was Evan. He didn't deserve to be mistreated, and he certainly didn't deserve to die. This is something that I imagine I will struggle with for the rest of my life.

I know that, someday, I will see Evan again. We will run to each other with open arms and hug each other tightly. All my pain and sadness will be gone, and all I will feel is peace and love. Only then will I understand what all of this was for. Until then, I am still a mother who is missing her son and longing for the day I can be with him again.

A Call to Action

What can you do? There are many things you can do to help me share Evan's story and save lives. Awareness and education are key. As parents, we try our very best to protect our children, but we can only protect them and educate them about the things we know about.

The first thing you can do is never say "not my child." If someone would have asked me if I thought my son would ever "play" the choking game, I would've said "no." Hundreds of other parents who lost their children this way would say the same thing. Now when I think about it, I can see why Evan did it. Evan was a very impulsive child due to his ADHD. He didn't always think before acting. Also, children at this age are more likely to be influenced by peer pressure. They want to fit in and are sometimes willing to do anything it takes to be accepted by their peers.

Even smart kids can make bad choices. They are still just children with brains that are not fully developed. They can't always think about things the way we do as adults with fully developed brains. Children tend to think that they are invincible and that nothing bad can happen to them. We need to talk to our children and have an open dialogue with them. You want them to feel safe to come and talk to you.

One of the most important things you can do is monitor their electronic usage. There are all kinds of things that they can be exposed to. While some of it can be good, a lot of it can be bad. There are tons of challenges on social media, including the deadly pass-out games. Kids tend to think, if they see other kids doing things in these videos without getting hurt, then they won't get hurt either. This couldn't be farther from the truth. Even if your children do not have social media, and you monitor their electronic usage, they still have friends and peers who do have it. As I mentioned earlier, my son did not have a cell phone or social media, and we did monitor his electronics, however, he was exposed to the pass-out challenge by a student at school.

You can also talk to your child's school and ask them to speak to the students about the deadly pass-out challenge and other social media challenges. Erik's Cause provides an excellent program that can be used in schools and it's easy enough for anyone to do. You can also ask the school to even send an email out to the parents making them aware of the challenge so they can talk to their children. If you are not sure what to say to your children or how to approach the subject, www.erikscause.org is an excellent source of information for parents and schools.

Please teach your children to be kind and accepting of others. We never know what someone else might be going through, and you could be the person who makes or breaks their day. Personally, I'd rather be the one who *makes* their day.

I have always told my kids to just be kind and follow the Golden Rule: If you wouldn't like someone to do it to you then don't do it to someone else. I have also taught them to stand up for themselves and for others.

Warrior on and fight for what you believe in. I know Evan did this, and I see Ava doing it too. One person may not be able to change the world, but you may be able to change the world for one person.

And always remember that Everyone is Valued, Accepted, and Needed.

Author Bio

After losing her son, Evan, in 2016 Dana Ziemniak has made it her mission to educate others and spread awareness about the deadly internet challenge that took her son's life and continues to take the lives of other children.

Because her son had ADHD, anxiety, and high-functioning autism, she is passionate about advocating for better support for children with disabilities in schools.

Dana lives in Pittsburgh, Pa., with her husband Matt and daughter Ava. She received a bachelor of science degree in pharmacy from Duquesne University and worked as a pharmacist in various settings for 15 years. She has been a full-time stay-at-home mom for over 10 years.

www.ingramcontent.com/pod-product-compliance
Lightning Source LLC
Chambersburg PA
CBHW071149120626
46546CB00006B/2182